Why It's Great to Be a Girl

ALSO BY JACQUELINE SHANNON

Young Adult Novels

Too Much T.J.
Upstaged
Big Guy, Little Women
Faking It
I Hate My Hero

Nonfiction

The New Mother's Body Book

Why It's Great to Be a Girl

❀

50 Eye-Opening Things You Can Tell Your Daughter to Increase Her Pride in Being Female

JACQUELINE SHANNON

WARNER BOOKS

A Time Warner Company

Warner Books, Inc., 1271 Avenue of the Americas, New York, NY 10020

W A Time Warner Company

Printed in the United States of America
First Printing: May 1994
10 9 8 7 6 5 4 3 2 1

Library of Congress Cataloging-in-Publication Data

Shannon, Jacqueline.
    Why it's great to be a girl : fifty eye-opening things you can
tell your daughter to increase her pride in being female /
Jacqueline Shannon.
        p.   cm.
    Includes bibliographical references.
    ISBN 0-446-39539-0
    1. Women—Miscellanea.   2. Sex differences—Miscellanea.
I. Title.
HQ1233.S48   1994
305.4—dc20   93-20923
                                                         CIP

Book design by Giorgetta Bell McRee
Cover design by Diane Luger
Cover illustration by Ruth Marten

For my own great little girl
Madeline Maria Trobaugh
Keep those questions coming, kid.
(And thanks for #40)

Many Thanks

. . . To my editor, Jamie Raab of Warner Books, and my agent, Lisa Bankoff of ICM, fellow mothers of young daughters, for their ideas and enthusiasm.

. . . To my first fantastic female role models: my mother, Louise Farmer, and my grandmother, the late Ruth Wroble. And to my dad, Dr. E. J. Farmer, who never once said "Girls can't/shouldn't do that."

. . . To my friends Roberta Lorbeer and Rachel McCurry for their early encouragement about the project; to Sharon Whitley, who listened patiently on our daily walks to my excited and incessant babbling about my research; and to Catherine Nicholas Cento for twenty-three years of assertiveness training.

. . . To A.D., my regular sparring partner, whose quaint discourses always sent me flying for the keyboard (and who is about to get an education in all that pen is mightier business).

. . . And to my husband, who read the manuscript without flinching, added valuable insights and suggestions, and—had I been allowed one—would have inspired a #51: *Because there are guys out there like Stephen Trobaugh to marry.*

Introduction

This book was inspired by the little girl I lost and the little girl I have now.

Try to picture the following scenarios:

• A four-year-old girl is telling a twelve-year-old neighbor about what she "shared" that day during circle time at preschool. "When you're my age," the older girl replies, "you don't get to share stuff; you just have to answer the teacher's questions. And it's usually the boys who do that." "Why?" the little girl asks. The older girl shrugs. "Maybe because the girls don't want to look too smart. Or maybe because the boys are just smarter."

• An elderly man walking his dog through a park stops to talk to a little girl climbing on the monkey bars. "When I grow up, I'm going to be a ballerina and a doctor," the girl tells the man. "You let the boys be the doctors," the man replies. "Girls don't have the stomach to deal with blood."

• A preschooler arrives home from a visit to a playmate's house one Sunday evening. "Mommy," she says, wide-eyed, "we watched '60 Minutes,' and they said when women in India find out they have girl babies in their tummies, they try to kill them because they want boys!"

Each of these incidents occurred in the same week of June 1993 . . . and in each case that little girl was my daughter Madeline. Sexism is still alive and living not just in faraway India but in my southern California neighborhood . . . and in yours.

As a parent or other concerned adult, what can you do about it? Obviously you cannot call the PC police. You cannot simply tell your daughter that all insensitive people are idiots (not when a distant relative or a close friend's mother is among the offenders). And unfortunately you can't be there to clamp your hands over your daughter's ears whenever someone starts a sentence with "Girls can't. . . ." But you have to do something. You have to deal with that hurt, puzzled look in your daughter's eyes. You have to keep that look from turning into one of acceptance . . . or even agreement.

What I've discovered works best is this: I *counteract* these doses of boy bias by building up Madeline's pride in her own gender. Here's one of my methods: Whenever she asks a gender-related question, I put a positive spin on the answer. For example, when she got around to asking the inevitable "Why don't I have a penis?" I said, "Nature was kinder to girls when it came to genital design. Ours are tucked safely inside, protected from getting cold or hurt."

And I counter any evidence she hears that boys are better at something with evidence of something at which *girls* excel—backed up by newspaper clippings, medical journal articles, and other sources I run across in my work as a journalist. Example: When she was three, Madeline came home from preschool and complained that the boys were bragging about how they're stronger than girls. "And they are, aren't they, Mommy?" she asked.

I nodded. "But during circle time, who answers the most questions?"

"Me," she said. "And Alyssa. And Staci." Then it dawned on her: "Are girls smarter than boys?"

"Girls are better with words than boys are."

Soon it occurred to me that I should be sharing such information with the parents of other little girls—parents who are thrilled to have those little girls. Parents who are not just thrilled to have them, but are well aware of the fact that the world their daughters will go out into as adults may very well still be a man's world. Parents who understand nevertheless that inoculating their daughters with shots of confidence from the start will enable them to compete better, even thrive in such a world.

There's proof of this. In 1992 the American Psychological Association held a symposium on the subject of "Gender, Power, and Leadership." At that meeting, researchers revealed that successful women politicians like Feinstein and Ferraro,

Boxer and Braun received five recurring messages throughout their early lives that inspired them to greatness. The messages: (1) you are loved and special, (2) you can do anything you want, (3) it's okay to take risks, (4) it's okay to enjoy and use your creative aggression, and (5) you can dream of greatness.

As I started to work on this book, my goal was to help parents deliver as many of these messages to their daughters as possible. It soon became clear that I could best do that by also including some role models; by covering not just the innate superiorities of females but some of our extraordinary accomplishments as well—accomplishments often made despite the discouragement, scorn, or even outright prohibition of society; accomplishments that benefited not just women but all of humankind.

Looking back on my own school history classes, I can honestly remember learning about only two women who were not wives of presidents. They were Pocahontas and Betsy Ross, and now it turns out that whole flag story was cooked up by Ross's grandson to get publicity for himself. Until I started researching this book, I had no idea that such revolutionary inventions as solar heating and computer programming were created by women. Nor did I know that a woman introduced kindergarten in America or that a woman is responsible for the fact that mentally ill people are no longer housed in prisons with criminals. The more I researched, the more astounded I became not only by the range of women's achievements but by the fact that most of this information is *still* not, as a rule, being taught in school. (I recently asked a twelve-year-old girl if she knew who Jane Addams was and she guessed "John Quincy Adams's mother?")

That girl could have been me. And this is where the little girl I lost comes in. I was something of a childhood star. I was the fastest runner in the entire first grade; skipped fourth grade and still managed to win the school spelling bee in fifth; won a first prize in the city science fair and edited a nationally award-winning edition of the school newspaper in ninth. But then something happened to me along about the time I turned fourteen. Although I can't remember any specific incidents that triggered it, I completely lost my self-confidence. I dropped out of athletics, refused a prestigious position on the high school yearbook staff, and basically skulked my way through high school and then college, too. About the only preadolescent activity I kept up was writing—mostly as a convenient vehicle for putting myself down—and I had what now appear to be fairly extraordinary career successes early on. I sold my first short story to a national magazine, for example, before I was out of high school. But for years—through my late teens and all of my twenties—I wrote off every publishing achievement like that to luck or to my assumption that someone didn't want to hurt my feelings by rejecting my work (a real hoot if you've ever had any dealings with the publishing world). I did not really get my old self-confidence back till I was past thirty. I am doing fine now, but I can't help but wonder: Where would I be now if my self-confidence hadn't taken an eighteen-year hiatus?

I wish I could say that my story is an unusual one, but clearly it parallels that of most teenage girls today. A 1991 American Association of University Women study found that only 29 percent of young teenage girls were "happy the way I am," compared to the 60 percent who gave that response back in elementary school . . . and in marked contrast to their teenage male counterparts, whose self-images have been judged much more positive. Carol Gilligan, who heads up Harvard's Project on the Psychology of Women and the Development of Girls, has found that one of the ways teenage girls exhibit their wavering confidence is by becoming more tentative in offering opinions—a trait that she says often persists into adulthood. A Gilligan example: When she interviewed one girl at age twelve, the girl answered "I don't know" only twenty-one times; at age fourteen, the same girl's "I don't know" number shot up to 135.

It is my hope that this book will find its way into the hands of both adults who are raising and teaching young girls and older girls whose self-esteem is beginning that plunge. If you are twelve or thirteen or fourteen and you've felt your confidence in yourself start to waver, *please read this book!* Check out how much you've got going for yourself. I promise you, by the time you get to point #50, you'll be in awe of what your gender has achieved, full of pride about the special talents and strengths of your female body and mind, and fully convinced, once and forever, that it really is great to be a girl.

—J.S.
Mammoth Mountain, California
1993

#1. Nature was kinder to females when it came to genital design. Yours are tucked safely inside, protected from cold and injury.

*I*t's the perfect answer to that inevitable question: "Why don't I have a penis?"

Here's the way one mother explained it to her seven-year-old daughter: "You've ridden a boy's ten-speed bicycle, right? And surely at least once you've accidentally slid off the seat and landed hard on the bar that connects it with the handlebars. You know that agony? Well, multiply that by ten and you've got a rough idea of what it feels like to a boy when he does that."

Here's Madonna on the subject: "I wouldn't want a penis. It would be like having a third leg. It would seem like a contraption that would get in the way."

And here's Mister Rogers: "Boys are fancy on the outside, girls on the inside." Be profoundly glad of that!

#2. While mostly males participate in the spectator or "watched" sports, overall, females are the most active athletes.

So say social forecasters Patricia Aburdene and John Naisbitt in *Megatrends for Women,* and so can you when your daughter gets around to asking on some Sunday afternoon, "Why do only men play in the sports we watch on TV?" The stats to back you up:

More than 65 percent of American women participate in sports or fitness activities, according to a 1991 *Sports Illustrated* poll. Women make up the majority of participants in six of seven of the most popular fitness activities—aerobics, walking, exercising with equipment, calisthenics, swimming, and bike riding. In cycling, basketball, running, and weight training, women make up the majority of new participants. In hiking and cross-country skiing—two of the hottest sports of the 1990s—women constitute the majority.

Since 1972, when Title IX forbade sex discrimination in schools that get federal funding, the number of girls participating in sports has skyrocketed. Today almost 2 million high school girls participate in interscholastic sports—a 500 percent increase over the 1972 total.

One last nugget: All five of the gold medals the United States brought home from the 1992 Winter Olympics were won by women.

#3. *Females invented many of the devices that make our everyday lives easier.*

The dishwasher, for example, plus disposable diapers, the bra, flat-bottomed paper bags, Scotchgard, and the drip coffee maker. But women inventors haven't limited themselves to hearth and home. The list of woman-born inventions also includes the bulletproof vest, the fire escape, the Navy's signal flare, the circular saw, solar heating, invisible glass, computer programming, DuPont's Kevlar (a thread that's as strong as steel), Liquid Paper typewriter correction fluid, pneumatic tires, and even the white line that divides a road. Going back a bit further in time, Greek scholars believe Queen Semiramis of Assyria invented bridges, causeways, and canals. During World War II, Hedy Lamarr (yes, the 1930s film star!) invented a sophisticated and hush-hush torpedo-control device to foil the Nazis, a device that now speeds satellite communications throughout the world. Ruth Handler, best known as the inventor of the Barbie Doll, also invented the first truly natural-looking breast prosthesis for mastectomy patients. More recently, Elsa Garmire, director of the University of Southern California Center for Laser Studies, developed a cost-effective method of zapping graffiti with a laser so that it simply evaporates.

Experts believe women invented scores of other useful contraptions we now take for granted, but never received credit for their work. Many women, especially those who did their inventing before 1900, registered patents under their husband's or father's name because (1) women had no property rights until the turn of the century, and (2) to be mechanical was considered unfeminine.

A case in point: Have you ever heard of Catherine Littlefield Greene? She was evidently behind the invention of a machine that changed the course of American history. In 1792 Greene, a widow with five children, was running a boarding-house in Georgia. When she became annoyed with the amount of time she had to spend separating cotton from its seeds so that she could spin it into thread, she prodded a young boarder named Eli Whitney to come up with a machine to do the work for her. With Greene's financial support, Whitney enthusiastically tackled the problem and after about six months came up with a prototype of the cotton gin, then almost gave up because the wooden teeth he had devised to separate the seeds from the cotton just weren't tough enough for the job. It was Greene who suggested he try wire teeth instead; the rest is history. And that's a conservative version of the story. Some accounts have Greene actually providing Whitney with the plans for the machine. Wherever the truth lies, it's fact that Greene didn't get in on the patent and that the machine had immense historical repercussions. It enabled the South to develop a thriving economy based on cotton, which necessitated the revival of the previously dying slave trade so that there would be enough labor to pick the enormous amount of cotton soon required to meet worldwide demand. And that increase in the importing and ownership of slaves would lead to the Civil War.

On a lighter note, a woman is also credited with having invented the ice cream cone. We don't know her name, just that she was a female companion of one Charles E. Menches, who, while attending the 1904 Louisiana Purchase Exposition in St. Louis, bought her an ice cream sandwich and a bunch of flowers. The resourceful lady rolled up one wafer of the sandwich to serve as a holder for the flowers, then rolled up the other wafer for the ice cream. The cone was born.

#4. When it comes to vision, females have several advantages over males.

We see better in the dark. We see more shades of red than males do. And we see more of the world in one glance than they do because we have wider peripheral vision. Females get the bigger picture because we have more receptor rods and cones at the back of the eyeball (the retina) than males do.

Females also have better visual memory than males. In one of many tests that have proved this, researchers asked both men and women to study a drawing that contained several unrelated objects, such as an elephant, a guitar, and so forth. Then the researchers replaced the drawing with a second one that contained all of the same objects as the first plus some additional items. Participants were asked to circle the objects that were in new locations and to cross out those that weren't in the first drawing. Women consistently outperformed men on this test. The same thing happened in another study in which men and women were asked to remember the locations of objects they'd seen on a particular laboratory desk top. In this case, women were 70 percent better than men at remembering what was where. (And, hey, for those of you who may have heard that the cards are stacked in favor of a certain other gender when it comes to spatial skills, anthropologist Helen Fisher categorizes this remember-the-objects talent as a *spatial* skill!)

Out in the real world, our superior visual memory makes us better than males at finding our way by remembering landmarks.

All of this leads researchers to speculate that we were granted this skill—or it evolved by necessity—because in prehistoric times it was females who went out and foraged for food for the tribe. Because there were no maps in those days (or at least there weren't any of the portable, Thomas Brothers variety) women needed keen visual memory skills in order to find their way home through the forest.

#5. *Overall, females are better drivers than males.*

You won't catch a police officer or an insurance agent uttering that old husbands' tale that "Women are lousy drivers." Why? Because statistics point to men being more of a threat behind the wheel. Sixty-three percent of all reported traffic accidents involve male drivers. Bolstering that statistic: In a survey of 1,000 adults, researchers found that 63 percent of the men—but only 40 percent of the women—had at some time been in an accident while driving. Also: 20 percent of the men in that survey had gotten a ticket, compared to 10 percent of the women; 10 percent of the men had been fined for speeding, compared to 5 percent of the women; and 9 percent of the men had been ticketed for illegal parking, compared to 5 percent of the women. Other telling evidence: In fully forty states, males under age twenty-four are charged more for auto insurance than females of similar age. Historically, say the insurance companies, young adult females are involved in far fewer accidents than young adult males. A 1993 survey taken by California's Office of Traffic Safety found that two-thirds of the group the surveyors call the "hard-core speeders"—the daredevils who routinely and with no qualms exceed the speed limit—are young males. And there are many more female school-bus drivers in America than males. School systems prefer to hire females because they are more patient, more responsible, and less inclined to take risks.

#6. *Females are better with words than males are.*

*T*his one's a natural should your daughter ask you why her male compatriots at preschool hit and push when they're angry instead of "using their words."

Girls begin to speak earlier than boys do and are better readers at school, speak more fluently, understand what is said better, use words better, and learn foreign languages more easily. This is true whether we live in Nepal, the Netherlands, or Nebraska. We retain this edge in communication ability throughout our lives. Here are the current theories about why this is so:

First, certain areas connecting the right and left sides of the brain are larger and contain more connections in females than in males, leading researchers to conclude that females use both sides of the brain more frequently than males do; female brains are simply better organized for communication between the two sides. The left side of the brain controls language and verbal ability while the right is involved with spatial perception. When called upon to perform a language-related task, females are better able to ignore the spatial perception priority of the right side of the brain in order to utilize the language skills on the left side.

Second, scientific tests have proved that when females are presented with a language problem we use not just the areas in the brain that males do but additional ones as well, including an area that is involved in the emotional comprehension and expression of language. Translation: It's easier for us to express our emotions.

Finally, anthropologist Helen E. Fisher, who wrote *Anatomy of Love,* considers the most compelling argument for women's verbal superiority to be its link to the female hormone estrogen. She says that in a recent study of 200 women of childbearing age, their verbal skills—such as the ability to repeat a tongue twister like "A box of mixed biscuits in a biscuit mixer"—peaked at midcycle, when estrogen levels are also at their highest. Right after menstruation, when levels are much lower, the women's tongue-twister skill declined (although even at their worst, the women generally beat the men at all verbal tasks).

Incidentally, scientists have acknowledged the superiority of female language skills for generations. Here, for example, in Canadian psychologist D. O. Hebb's ancient (1958) *A Textbook of Psychology,* is a snappy rejoinder to guys who discount the value of female verbal talent: "Males, who are inclined to think that verbal skill is due simply to talking too much, may be reminded that language is man's distinguishing mark as a species."

BONUS!

*Females hold on to their verbal skills longer
than males do.*

According to a 1991 University of Pennsylvania study, males probably lose their verbal abilities faster than females. Using magnetic resonance imaging—a kind of X ray without the radiation—researchers studied the brains of thirty-four men and thirty-five women. They found that deterioration in the brain—especially in the left side, which controls language and verbal ability—was two to three times faster in men. How do the researchers account for that? They speculate that our female hormones "may protect the brain from atrophy associated with aging." Previous studies have shown that these hormones increase blood flow to the brain—that may be what's providing the protection.

But just what does the faster deterioration of men's verbal abilities mean? That old men forget what they wanted to say more frequently than old women?

That they have more trouble coming up with that word that's "right on the tip of my tongue"? Stay tuned. That's what the researchers are working on now—how changes in the brain affect changes in behavior.

#7. Females are also superior at nonverbal communication.

*T*hat is, females are better at sensing the difference between what people say and what they mean. We're better at reading other people's emotional clues—for example, the facial wince, nervous hand clenching, and other subconscious signals that we might put together to conclude that a person is feeling guilty.

Mother Nature probably bestowed this skill on females so that we can better mother infants who aren't yet able to communicate their needs verbally. Like language ability, the skill is attributed to the particular setup, patterns, and interactions of the feminine brain . . . making "women's intuition" a scientific reality.

Interestingly, psychologist Joyce Brothers believes that it's this skill that will eventually make females the dominant gender. She predicts that, in the future, physical strength—which has kept males dominant until now—may become about as necessary as the appendix is today.

"The key to survival in the nuclear age is going to be perception, the ability to sense how others feel about an event or an issue or a threat and what they are likely to do about it," she wrote in *What Every Woman Should Know About Men*. "Everyone can think of episodes in our foreign policy that illustrate a serious lack of perception. As more women enter government and politics at the higher policy-making levels, I am convinced there will be fewer such episodes."

BONUS!

Females are able to make up their minds faster than males.

Researchers believe females can make faster decisions because we more frequently put *both* sides of our brains to work on a problem. Here's how Phil Donahue once explained it in his book *The Human Animal*: "Think of the brain as a city divided in half by a river. In the female brain, because there are many more bridges over the river, traffic moves faster and more efficiently between the two halves."

#8. *Anthropologists and archeologists credit females with the "civilization" of humankind.*

As Elizabeth Gould Davis put it in her book *The First Sex,* "Women dragged man, kicking and screaming, out of savagery into the New Stone Age." How? According to Buckminster Fuller, "Women organized the home crew to pound the corn, thresh the grain, comb the wool, dry the skins, etc. They invented pottery and weaving, discovered how to keep foods by cold storage or by cooking. Women, in fact, invented industrialization."

We're also credited with beginning the domestication of animals and—most important of all—with inventing agriculture. "While [man] enjoyed himself, [women] observed that the seeds dropped on the midden pile produced newer and bigger plants," wrote Kenneth MacGowan and Joseph A. Hester, Jr., in *Early Man in the New World.* Out of the invention of agriculture, the authors continued, "rose a settled community and a surplus of provender which allowed the few . . . to think and plan and build civilization." MacGowan and Hester believe that woman also invented milling stones to grind seeds, and they speculate that "as she watched the wearing away of mortar and pestle and milling stone as she ground her flour between them the idea occurred to her . . . that it was possible to grind stones into axes and other implements." If that was true, we can also pat ourselves on the back for inventing manufacture!

What motivated us to be so inventive? Davis believes it was because woman has eternally struggled "to make the best of things, to provide food and shelter for her children, to make 'home' comfortable for them, to soften and brighten their lives, and to make the world a safer and more pleasant place for them to grow in."

#9. *Females smell better than males.*

We're talking b.o. here. The human sweat gland is called the apocrine gland—and there are hundreds of these in the human armpit, scientifically known as the axillary. "Sure there are some first-class women stinkers," said Albert Kligman, a University of Pennsylvania professor of dermatology, in *Health* magazine. But, added Kligman, who was coauthor of a dermatology journal article entitled "Perspectives on Axillary Odor," the apocrine gland is androgen-driven. Androgens are male hormones, though women have some, too. "Men have more androgen and bigger apocrine glands, and they stink more," according to Kligman. (Trivia file: That is, unless they're Asian men. Kligman said Asians have few aprocrine glands. In Japan, in fact, b.o. is considered a medical problem that, until just a few years ago, even merited discharge from the Imperial Japanese Army.)

Compounding the problem is the fact that males aren't as aware as females are of whether or not they smell because . . .

#10. *Females also smell better than males!*

Women are more sensitive to odors than men are. A 1985 test of some 2,000 noses at the Smell and Taste Center at the Hospital of the University of Pennsylvania is one of several studies that prove it. Interestingly, the smelling ability of females actually gets even better once we're through puberty. Researchers tie this skill to female hormones . . . specifically, estrogen. When estrogen levels are highest—at ovulation— a woman's smell sensitivity can increase up to a whopping 1,000 times. Because of the hormonal tie, it seems obvious Mother Nature felt superschnozzes were somehow needed for reproductive purposes. It's been proven to a statistically scientific degree that mothers of six-hour-old babies can find their own baby among a group of others by smell alone while males cannot.

A corroborating anecdote: A residential repair worker at San Diego Gas & Electric tells customers to always trust a woman's nose. "I've seen heated arguments between husband and wife—she says she smells gas, he insists that he doesn't," the repairman said recently. "In my fifteen years on the job, the woman has been right every single time."

BONUS!

Female voices don't "crack" during puberty.

When a boy's voice begins to deepen during puberty, he has to go through an embarrassing stage when his voice can crack or even squeak without warning. Oftentimes, it happens at the worst possible moment, the moment of high stress, such as when he's asked to answer a question in class. What's happening is that his vocal cords have begun to double in size and he has to relearn how to control the pitch of the sound they produce. Yes, female vocal cords increase in size and our voices change during puberty, too. But, according to medical experts, the increase in size is only about 30 percent, and the change is much more smooth and gradual—nothing, as a writer for *'Teen* magazine once put it, to "crack up" about.

#11. *Some of history's most effective and powerful leaders have been queens.*

A nice "but" to add after you've had to tell your daughter, "No, there has never been a female president of the United States."

Poland's Queen Jadwiga (1373–1399), for example, is considered one of that country's greatest rulers as well as one of the truly inspired peacemakers of history, according to anthropologist Ashley Montagu. "England's Queen Elizabeth I and Victoria rank among the greatest of English monarchs," he added in his book *The Natural Superiority of Women.*

When Elizabeth I became queen in the sixteenth century, England was in a horrible state. The country had just lost a war against France, the royal treasury was depleted, and England's citizens, hostile and resentful after Mary Tudor's bloody and bigoted reign, were still fighting with each other over the question of England's religion: Was the country Catholic or Protestant? When Elizabeth died, England was the richest and most powerful country in the world. During the golden years of her reign—dubbed the Elizabethan Age in her honor—the country became the "Mistress of the Seas" by defeating the Spanish Armada and expanded its trading and holdings throughout the world. Elizabeth was also the monarch who made the Church of England the country's official religion.

The reign of Queen Victoria was also an era of extreme prosperity and prestige for England. In fact, some historians consider the late 1890s—when Victoria was celebrating sixty years on the throne—to be the time the country was at its peak of power. Supposedly, when Victoria died England's citizens were so grief stricken that all of the stores sold out of black cloth.

Russia's Catherine the Great (1729–1796) reigned over that country's pre-Revolution expansion into one of the world's major powers. She added the Crimea, the Ukraine, Lithuania, and Poland to the Russian empire. Some of the many social reforms she instituted include establishing free hospitals and schools throughout the country, building new towns, highways, and canals, promoting religious tolerance, reforming the tax system, standardizing the laws and the currency so that they no longer differed among the Russian provinces, and improving the living and working conditions of the serfs.

Queen Isabella was at the helm when Spain first reached the world leadership position it would hold in the 1400s and 1500s. She united the splintered country, and because of that and its growing number of colonies in the New World, Spain became for a time the most powerful country in Europe.

And during the sixteenth-century reign of Queen Catherine

de Medici, writes Elizabeth Gould Davis in *The First Sex*, "France rose to her status as the cultural and intellectual center of the world—a status maintained down to our own time."

Marveling at the success of queens, one eighteenth-century male scholar speculated that the "lenity and moderation" of females make us "fitter for good administration than [the] severity and roughness" of you know who.

#12. *Two females initiated the discovery and colonization of the land that would become the United States of America.*

*T*wo of the above-mentioned queens, as a matter of fact.

True, the Indians were in America first, but Europeans have always gotten the credit for "discovering" and colonizing the United States as we now know it. And the first of those—Christopher Columbus—was able to go for it only because Spain's Queen Isabella gave him the money he needed for his trip. While other higher-ups in Spain wrote off as impossible the idea that the confident but penniless Columbus could sail directly west to reach the Indies—instead of taking the usual route around the tip of Africa—Isabella believed so strongly in Columbus that she pledged her crown jewels to finance the expedition.

In 1578, fifty-four years after Isabella died, England's Queen Elizabeth I, who was far more interested in exploring the new land than her grandfather (Henry VII) or her father (Henry VIII) had been, issued the first patent for English colonization of the New World's mainland. In issuing this patent, Elizabeth stipulated that no Englishman would lose his citizenship rights by moving to the New World. It was this assurance that encouraged thousands of English citizens to head west over the next 200 years, ultimately resulting in the birth of the United States.

#13. *Females currently hold the highest office in several countries of the world.*

*I*t's another factor to point out when your disappointed little girl discovers that there's never been a female president of the United States.

Take Ireland and Iceland, for example. Mary Robinson was elected president of Ireland in 1990 with 52.8 percent of the vote, despite the fact that oddsmakers had initially predicted the odds as 100 to 1 against her. In Iceland, Vigdis Finnbogadottir has been elected president four times since 1980. The extremely popular president has garnered as much as 95 percent of the votes.

More recently, in 1993, Kim Campbell was elected leader of Canada's ruling Progressive Conservative Party, a position that automatically made her the country's prime minister (and the first female to head a government in North America). Also in 1993, Tansu Ciller became the first female prime minister of Turkey, despite the fact that the country is predominantly Islamic, a religion that traditionally discourages women from assuming leadership roles. In 1991, a woman named Begum Khaleda Zia was elected prime minister of Bangladesh, another Islamic country. And in 1992, Hanna Suchocka was voted prime minister of Poland, a first for females there.

Violeta Barrios de Chamorro became war-torn Nicaragua's first democratically elected official in almost 200 years when in 1990 she stunned the world by defeating Daniel Ortega in the presidential election.

The indisputable champion when it comes to female leadership is Norway. Not only does that country have a female prime minister—Gro Harlem Brundtland—but all three of Norway's biggest political parties are also headed by women.

The Philippines might still be headed by Corazon Aquino, who energized the populace after they'd lived twenty-one years under the rule of Ferdinand and Imelda Marcos, had she not been constitutionally limited to a six-year term as president.

Two other women left the highest offices of their respective countries in the early 1990s. In 1992, Edith Cresson, who had become France's first female prime minister in 1991, resigned after her political party pulled in only 18 percent of the vote in regional elections. Great Britain's Margaret Thatcher—the most famous and influential female prime minister of our time—was put out of office by her own Conservative party in 1990 after an almost unprecedented three consecutive terms. Thatcher had been prime minister since 1979. According to the *Washington Post*, a whole generation of British kids was brought up so accustomed to the idea of a female leading their country that when Conservatives chose John Major to replace

Thatcher, a child asked, "But Daddy, can a *man* be prime minister?"

And there's hope for America. Social forecasters Patricia Aburdene and John Naisbitt have predicted in *Megatrends for Women* that we'll have our first woman president by 2008. They say women are being elected to more and more local and state offices, the stepping-stones to the big ones. For example, 19 of the 100 largest cities in the United States have female mayors.

According to the Center for the American Woman and Politics at Rutgers University, women made historic gains in the U.S. Congressional races in 1992, the election year labeled "The Year of the Woman." The number of women in the U.S. Senate doubled from three to six (and a seventh was added after a special Texas election in 1993). A record-breaking 104 women ran for House seats in 1992, and 47 won them, upping the old House total of 28 by 19 seats. "Public opinion polls," said pollster Celinda Lake in the *Chicago Tribune*, "showed that voters overwhelmingly believed that women . . . could make government work for ordinary people."

#14. *The most frequently sung song of all time was written by females.*

Mildred Hill and Patty Smith Hill wrote "Happy Birthday to You" in 1893. It became the first song ever sung in space (at least by earthlings!) on March 8, 1969, when the astronauts aboard *Apollo IX* sang it for Christopher Kraft, director of space operations for NASA. Contrary to popular belief, "Happy Birthday" is not in the public domain. Hill set up a foundation to which a royalty is supposed to be paid for each entertainment usage of the song—when it's sung on a sitcom, for example.

Incidentally, a woman, Euphemia Allen, also composed what is probably the song played most often on the piano—"Chopsticks"!

Speaking of musical achievement . . .

#15. *Females sing better than males.*

Six times as many females as males can sing in tune. Why? No expert claims to have the definitive answer. But most speculate that better singing is a part of the female's superior verbal-ability package (see #6). Others point to the fact that females have superior auditory memory (see #28)—that is, we are better at remembering the way a song is supposed to sound, say from hearing it on the radio. It probably also doesn't hurt that mothers tend to sing more to girl babies than to boy babies, according to some studies.

#16. *Except for muscles, the female body is stronger than the male body in every way.*

Women have greater stamina and energy. We live longer, are less susceptible to the major diseases, and are more likely to recover from those diseases if we get them.

The life expectancy of a baby girl born today is 83.25 years, for a baby boy 74.4 years. Of the 35,800 Americans who were 100 years old or more at the 1990 census, 28,000 were female. Part of the reason women live longer is that we smoke less, drink less, and take fewer life-threatening chances than men do. But we also tend to be less vulnerable to mortal illnesses like cancer and heart disease. Researchers used to attribute that to the fact that men—who went out to the workplace every day while women stayed home—were under more stress, which is believed to be a contributor to many fatal diseases. But many more women are out in the work force today than in decades past—the percentage of employed women in the United States nearly doubled between 1950 and 1985—and researchers are finding that working women are just as healthy as their counterparts who stay home.

It now appears that Mother Nature, once again, favored women. Scientists are pointing to female hormones as one key to the puzzle. One of the duties of estrogen, the "female" hormone, is to keep a woman's blood vessels pliable so they'll be able to accommodate extra blood volume during pregnancy. A happy side benefit of this is that it reduces our risk of developing atherosclerosis, the clogging of the arteries that is the cause of coronary heart disease. Also, because a fetus would need plenty of carbohydrates but little fat, estrogen helps the body to break down excess fat by stimulating the liver to produce HDL (high-density lipoproteins), also known as the "good" cholesterol. HDL, which enables the body to make more efficient use of fat, also helps to keep the arteries clear of LDL (low-density lipoproteins), also known as the "bad" cholesterol.

How valuable are these safeguards? Look at the numbers: A twenty-four-year study of the health of nearly 6,000 men and women ages thirty to fifty-nine found about twice the incidence of heart disease in the men as in the women, even in the upper age range, where women have less estrogen than their younger counterparts. Before women hit menopause, we are four times less prone to heart attacks than men are.

Testosterone, the male hormone, seems to be responsible for decreasing a male's HDL, or "good" cholesterol, while raising his level of LDL, or "bad" cholesterol. Testosterone, which is responsible for aggressiveness and is also known as "frogs and snails and puppy dogs' tails," seems to have "hung on past its glory days," as Edward Dolnick put it in *In Health* magazine. "[It] may have been a nifty innovation when men's major duty was hurling rocks at the next tribe. But testosterone doesn't seem like a bargain anymore—since today we hunt only if someone has misplaced the remote-control clicker."

Another key to the puzzle may be the intriguing and mounting evidence linking heart disease with the amount of iron a person eats and then stores in the body. Contrary to popular belief—"Eat your meat! It's chockful of iron to keep you healthy!"—the more iron you store, the higher your risk of a heart attack may be. One Finnish study of 1,900 men, in fact, showed that high iron levels are second only to smoking when it comes to heart-attack risk factors. The typical female of childbearing age has only a third as much iron stored as her male counterpart. Why? Because when we menstruate each month, we lose a significant amount of iron. What our grandmothers once called "the curse" looks very much like a blessing!

Another advantage Mother Nature bestowed upon females is more body fat. On average, men have 15 percent body fat while women have 23 pecent. Fat is the body's fuel, and the 8 percent more that women have stashed away gives us more energy and stamina than men have. And that's one of the major reasons that women survive physically stressful situations, such as being shipwrecked, better than men do and that . . . well, take a quick peek ahead to #48.

BONUS!

Female muscles may not be as strong as male muscles, but they definitely have their advantages.

Male muscles are "striated"—meaning they have a high fiber content. Female muscles are smooth and less fibrous. "[Men's] striated muscles use energy in a less efficient manner than women's," says Joe Tanenbaum in *Male and Female Realities*. "Striated muscles allow immediate use of strength, but burn energy (that is, generate more heat) faster, thereby depleting the body's reserves more quickly." In fact, researchers in Atlanta recently concluded that just having more muscle mass *period* generates more heat and thus puts males at a disadvantage in endurance contests like marathons. That additional muscle-spawned heat makes men sweat more and therefore causes them to lose sodium and potassium, which play important roles in regulating body processes, faster than women do.

And there's more. Female muscles seem to be more adaptable to changes in the body. "Women's muscles have to adapt to a changing menstrual cycle with varied levels of hormones and water retention at different times of the month," according to *Parents* magazine. "Men's muscles are used to a relatively more stable environment—and so are more easily thrown for a loop when illness strikes, perhaps explaining why men complain of aches and pain more frequently when they get the flu." The magazine adds that the muscles of women are less likely to build up pain inducers than those of men. The result? Women may persevere on a task after men have given up because of the pain.

#17. A female personally led more American slaves to freedom than anyone else.

*H*er name was Harriet Tubman, and she was the most famous and successful "conductor" on the Underground Railroad—the secret routes slaves took from their homes in the South to the free states in the North. An escaped slave herself, Tubman led 300 slaves to freedom—in nineteen round-trips over ten years—via nighttime treks through swamps and forests that were heavily patrolled by slave catchers who'd been lured into the business by the hefty reward the slave owners offered. A $40,000 reward—a fortune in those days—was set on Tubman herself because her feats so enraged southern slave owners. The reward was for her capture dead or alive; had she been caught she most likely would have been put to death on the spot, and she knew it. She never lost a "passenger."

Nicknamed "Moses" because she, like her biblical counterpart, led her people out of slavery, Tubman served as an unofficial spy and scout for the North during the Civil War. Organizing black troops for the Union Army, she became their commanding officer. On June 2, 1863, she led them on a raid up South Carolina's Combahee River, setting fire to plantations, Confederate warehouses, and arsenals, and freeing another 800 slaves plus 500 prisoners of war along the way. Tubman's planning and execution of the mission were so perfect that not one of her troops was even injured, let alone killed.

Tubman accomplished all of this despite the fact that when she was a teenage slave, an overseer threw an iron weight at her for interfering with his capture of an escaping slave and it fractured Tubman's skull. The injury gave her periodic fainting spells for the rest of her life.

While we're on the subject of the War Between the States . . .

#18. More than any other factor, a book written by a female incited the Civil War, the war that ended slavery in America.

*T*he writer was Harriet Beecher Stowe and the book was *Uncle Tom's Cabin.* When Abraham Lincoln met her during the Civil War, he remarked, "So this is the little lady who started this big war." There's ample evidence that he wasn't kidding.

Stowe, both the daughter and wife of Protestant ministers, first became interested in the issue of slavery when she lived in Cincinnati, a station on the Underground Railroad, and made visits across the Ohio River to Kentucky, a slave state. She saw the slave system in practice on one side of the river and heard the stories of escaped slaves on the other. That input, along with *An Appeal in Favor of That Class of Americans Called Africans* and other antislavery books and articles in circulation in the North at that time, provided her with a wealth of information from which to draw her fictional characters and plot.

The hero of the overly melodramatic tale, which was first published as a serial in an antislavery newspaper, is the saintly Uncle Tom. In telling his story and the stories of several other slaves, Stowe covered in horrifying detail such realities of slavery as being sold at auction, being separated from one's children, and being forced to have sex. In the book's ending—which Stowe wrote first—Uncle Tom is beaten to death by his cruel master, Simon Legree, because he refuses to provide information about two escaped slaves.

Stowe apparently hoped to *avert* a war with her book. According to letters and other material written by and about her, Stowe's major goal was to reconcile the differences between the North and South. In a letter she wrote to a friend, she said she hoped, for example, that her book would moderate the bitterness of extremist abolitionists. She also wanted to inspire more compassion for blacks throughout the country. Convinced that her main audience would be southerners, she believed she portrayed the South fairly. For example, she made sure to include a few kind and compassionate slave owners in the story.

Stowe was stunned when the South reacted to her book with a storm of protest and hatred. She got thousands of furious letters from southerners, including one letter that included the cut-off ear of a slave. Some southern courts imposed long prison sentences on anyone caught with the book, and numerous southern authors wrote their own books that they claimed presented slavery as it really was.

But more important in the long run was the reaction to the book in the North. By 1860 *Uncle Tom's Cabin*, which had been published in 1851 (and had sold 2.5 million copies worldwide in that first year alone), had turned huge numbers of northerners into rabid haters of slavery, and made them ready and willing to go to war over the practice. Author Robert B. Downs, who included *Uncle Tom's Cabin* in his *Books That Changed America,* implies that, at the very least, the book hastened the Civil War by several years. Downs bolsters the argument that the book was in fact a major cause of the war by quoting "loyal Southerner" Thomas Nelson Page, who spent his childhood during the Civil War on a Virginia plantation and was later the U.S. ambassador to Italy and a novelist who critics said idealized plantation life. According to Page, "By arousing the general sentiment of the world against slavery, the novel contributed more than any other one thing to its abolition in that generation [and] did more than any one thing that ever occurred to precipitate the war."

The book was eventually translated into twenty-three languages. Stowe was visited and lauded by Mark Twain, thanked for her "good work" by England's Queen Victoria, and told that *Uncle Tom's Cabin* was one of the "great achievements of the human mind" by Russian novelist Leo Tolstoy.

Stowe herself put her money where her mouth was. With some of the royalties she earned from the book, she bought slaves and then freed them.

While the Civil War gave black Americans their freedom, it didn't grant them equality. That discrepancy would simmer for nearly a hundred years, until . . .

#19. *The courageous act of one female triggered the momentous civil rights movement of the 1960s.*

On December 1, 1955, a forty-two-year-old black woman named Rosa Parks boarded a city bus in Montgomery, Alabama. Parks, a seamstress active in the local branch of the National Association for the Advancement of Colored People (NAACP), was weary from her day's work. As required by Alabama's racial segregation laws, she took a seat in the back of the bus; the front was always reserved for whites. Soon the white section was full, and the bus driver "expanded" it to include the row Parks was sitting in. The driver ordered Parks to relinquish her seat to a white man. Parks had argued with bus drivers over this practice in the past, and one time she'd been thrown off a bus because she refused to use the rear door—another requirement. These incidents had given Parks a reputation as a troublemaker among the city's bus drivers, and many would drive right past her without stopping if they saw her standing alone at a bus stop.

On this particular December day, Parks was fed up with the humiliation and unfairness of not just the bus rules but of all of the segregation laws in the South that were designed to keep black people apart from and inferior to whites. She refused to give up her seat. "I knew someone had to take the first step," she later told a reporter. "I felt it was the right time and opportunity to let it be known that I didn't think I was treated right. If I hadn't done it then, I would have found some other way to make my feelings and desires known."

Parks was arrested for violating segregation laws. Her arrest infuriated local blacks. In response, they staged a bus boycott that lasted for more than a year and nearly bankrupted the bus company. The boycott solidified the black community . . . and also brought a young minister named Martin Luther King, Jr., into the spotlight. The subsequent crusades of King, Parks, and other black activists eventually resulted in the federal Civil Rights Act of 1957, the federal Voting Rights Act of 1965, and several Supreme Court decisions—including one in Parks's case that made bus segregation illegal. Together, these actions put an end to official segregation in the South.

#20. *Females are especially well suited to be doctors.*

*T*his is particularly true from a patient's point of view. Female physicians treat their patients more like equals than male doctors do. According to numerous studies, female doctors are more respectful, spend a lot more time with each patient, and interrupt that patient less frequently than their male counterparts. Recent evidence also suggests that female doctors just as readily embrace new medical technology and aggressive medical treatments. Add all of this up and you'll have to agree with Janet Bickel of the Association of Medical Colleges, who said in *The American Woman 1990–91*: "If women keep bringing these qualities into the practice of medicine, their increasing number is clearly good news for patients."

And the number of women doctors is, happily, increasing rapidly. While only 17 percent of today's physicians are women, females make up about 40 percent of the current enrollment in medical schools overall, and in some schools the percentage exceeds 50 percent.

Geneticist Ann Moir and writer David Jessel, who together

wrote *Brain Sex: The Real Difference Between Men and Women,* say that our "superiority in sensitivity and verbal ability" probably makes us not just better doctors than men, but better priests, legislators, and judges as well.

BONUS!

Females also make better astronauts.

When First Lady Hillary Rodham Clinton was twelve years old, she supposedly wrote to NASA asking how she could be an astronaut. NASA responded that she did not qualify because of her gender.

Well, according to Phil Donahue, if astronauts had been chosen from the start based on their biological credentials alone, it would have been the *other* gender that couldn't qualify. Why? Because females are smaller, weigh less, need less oxygen and food, are generally healthier, and handle stress better. Also, our eyes are better at picking tiny objects (for example, stars) out of a large field (for example, outer space). A male may have been first to set foot on the moon, but the first human being on Mars may be female, concludes Donahue in his book *The Human Animal.*

#21. Females have written many of our most enduring books.

Take Louisa May Alcott's *Little Women* (1868), for example, whose brave and brainy Jo March was 100 years ahead of her time. Other standouts: Emily Brontë's tale of the ultimate dysfuctional relationship in the passionate *Wuthering Heights* (1847), and her sister Charlotte's *Jane Eyre* (also published in 1847), the story of a Cinderella with guts. Jane Austen wrote *Pride and Prejudice* (1813); Mary Ann Evans (writing under the name George Eliot!) penned *The Mill on the Floss* (1860) and *Silas Marner* (1861). Swiss writer Johanna Spyri was lauded for her "insight into a child's mind" when she published *Heidi* in 1880. Edith Wharton wrote *Ethan Frome* (1911) and *The Age of Innocence* (1920), both of which became movies of the 1990s. A woman, Margaret Mitchell, created the most popular heroine in American fiction, Scarlett O'Hara, in *Gone with the Wind* (1936), and Harriet Beecher Stowe, who wrote the antislavery novel *Uncle Tom's Cabin,* probably incited the Civil War (see #18), the war that altered Scarlett's life—and Scarlett herself—forever. In 1934, P. L. Travers began her *Mary Poppins* series, creating a character "who proved that you can be an independent, strong-willed, and authoritarian woman without being a bitch," according to one of today's screenwriters for Disney, the studio that turned the series into a wildly successful movie in 1964.

Pearl Buck got a 1932 Pulitzer Prize for *The Good Earth*, about a poor Chinese couple and their struggle to achieve wealth. Other Pulitzer winners were Harper Lee (in 1961) for *To Kill a Mockingbird*, an early plea for racial justice, and (posthumously) Anne Frank, who, in her diary, wrote of her hope of living on after her death through her writing, but who certainly couldn't have imagined the scope to which she would do just that.

Incidentally, the first-ever novel, *The Tale of Genji*, was written by a woman, Lady Murasaki Shikibu, in eleventh-century Japan. The best-selling novel of all time was also written by a woman. According to the *Guinness Book of Records*, Jacqueline Susann's *Valley of the Dolls* has sold more than 28 million copies since it was published in 1967.

#22. *It was thanks to the efforts of a female that most Americans obtained the right to vote.*

*H*ere's how the Organization for Equal Education of the Sexes (OEES) puts it: While George Washington helped win the vote for fewer than 2 million white males and Abraham Lincoln helped win the vote for fewer than 1 million black males, Susan B. Anthony helped win the vote for 26 million American women. While she wasn't among those who made the *first* demand for votes for women (which happened in 1848), and she wasn't alive to see women finally cast ballots in a national election (in 1920), no one worked harder than Anthony to win that right. From 1851 until she died in 1906, she made this cause her only employment and the main focus of her life, according to the OEES. Her energy, determination, and executive ability are what held together the suffrage movement—which was subject to much of its own political infighting—for more than fifty years.

Anthony was born in 1820 into a Quaker community, which in those days treated women with far more equality than the rest of society. She set her sights on a teaching career and spent ten years in the profession, earning $2.50 a week. After growing dissatisfied with teaching—and full of outrage that male teachers earned significantly more money—Anthony quit and turned her attention to politics. She became active in the temperance (anti-alcohol) and antislavery movements. In the course of this work, she met Elizabeth Cady Stanton, who would become her primary partner in the long quest for the right to vote.

When they met, Stanton was already active in the women's rights movement, having organized the first American women's rights convention in Seneca Falls, New York, in 1848. She had little trouble converting Anthony to her cause, since Anthony had experienced so much discrimination herself, not just as a teacher but in the temperance movement as well. At temperance conventions, as at teachers meetings, women were not allowed to express their opinions before the crowd.

The collaboration of Anthony and Stanton was perfect: Stanton was an accomplished writer, and Anthony became a powerful and effective public speaker of Stanton's words. As Stanton's husband, Henry, once put it to his wife, "You stir up Susan and she stirs up the world."

Anthony was also fantastically successful at recruiting others to the cause and then inspiring them to work for it as doggedly as she did. Anthony herself was able to work ceaselessly because she was unmarried and childless, unlike Stanton, who had seven children.

In 1868 Anthony and Stanton began publishing a weekly newspaper (the *Revolution*) devoted to the women's rights battle, and in 1869 they founded the first American organization (the National Woman Suffrage Association) devoted solely to getting the vote for women. Anthony then spent the next thirty years on the road, keeping to an exhausting schedule of meetings and lectures—at which most of the audience had never before heard a woman speak in public—designed to win converts to her cause. Averaging 75 to 100 speeches a year, she did, in fact, change the national attitude about votes for women. In 1878 Anthony's friend, Senator A. A. Sargent of California, introduced into Congress the Susan B. Anthony Amendment, which would grant women the right to vote throughout the United States. But because most politicians were nowhere near as enlightened as Sargent, the amendment would not become law for another forty-two years.

Long before that, Anthony died. Did she die full of self-pity that she would not live to see women get the right she had fought so long for? No way. She died full of optimism. Shortly before her friend and colleague Stanton died in 1902, Anthony wrote to her about the younger, more radical generation of suffragists emerging on the scene and assured Stanton that she had "not a shadow of a doubt that they will carry our cause to victory." And just three weeks before her own death in 1906, a seriously ill Anthony—she'd had a stroke—made a speech at the annual suffrage convention in which she asserted, "I have never lost my faith, not for a moment. Failure is impossible."

And she was right. The Susan B. Anthony Amendment was signed into law in 1920, exactly 100 years after Anthony was born.

#23. *Females have better balance than males do.*

*I*t's because with our narrower shoulders and wider hips, we have a lower center of gravity. This advantage gives us increased stability for diving and makes us tougher to tackle in football—size being equal, of course—and, when combined with our greater flexibility and grace, makes us superior to males in figure skating and gymnastics, especially in floor exercise and on the balance beam.

BONUS!

Females have a longer attention span than males.

Psychologist Diane McGuinness of the University of South Florida has conducted numerous studies of gender differences in preschool children. In one study, she found that in a twenty-minute interval, girls started and *finished* more projects than boys. The boys

---

were simply more distractible—they stopped their play to look at something else four times more often than girls. They also spent more time watching other kids.

#24. Many of the greatest reforms to the American way of life were instigated by females.

*J*ust a few examples:

In the mid-1800s, a teacher named Dorothea Dix volunteered to teach a Sunday school class at a prison and was horrified to discover that mentally ill people were imprisoned along with criminals because there was nowhere else to keep them. She embarked on a ten-year crusade to reform the U.S. penal system and the care of the mentally ill. Traveling some 30,000 miles, she visited hundreds of state prisons and city jails, lectured widely, drafted legislation, worked with the state legislatures in nearly every state of the Union, and provided a detailed program for reform. She also worked to make treatment more constructive and humane at mental institutions. There were only thirteen such facilities when Dix began her crusade; by 1880, there were 123, thanks to her efforts, and she had personally designed and founded thirty-five of them. She also took her ideas abroad, sparking reform in country after country she visited.

Also in the 1800s, sisters Sarah and Angelina Grimke—white women who grew up on a South Carolina slave plantation—were leaders in the movement to abolish slavery, along with Elizabeth Cady Stanton and Lucretia Mott. Once that was accomplished, all four went on to prominence in America's first women's rights movement, in which women sought such basic freedoms as being allowed to vote, to attend college, to get custody of their children after a divorce, to keep their own earnings, and to own property. Before the Civil War, the legal status of an American wife was comparable to that of a slave in the South.

In 1871, a few years after she lost her husband and all four of her children to an epidemic of yellow fever and then lost her dressmaking business in the great Chicago fire, Mary Harris Jones became obsessed with the plight of American workers. In many industries, wages were piddling and working conditions were deplorable and dangerous. For the next fifty years, despite being mobbed, beaten, and imprisoned, Mother Jones (as she became known) organized workers, especially miners, into fledgling labor unions that pushed for improved pay and working conditions.

In the last years of the nineteenth century, Jane Addams, a woman from a wealthy family, became appalled at the conditions of the city slums that were teeming with immigrants. Some of her complaints, in her own words: "Unsanitary housing, poisonous sewage, contaminated water, infant mortality, the spread of contagion, adulterated food, impure milk, smoke-laden air, ill-ventilated factories, dangerous occupations, juvenile crime, [and] unwholesome crowding. . . ." She decided to borrow the British idea of "settlement houses" for America, and established one in Chicago. Her Hull House became the model for settlement houses all over the world. Settlement house workers helped immigrants become established in America, for example, by teaching them English. But they also pressured city administrators to improve conditions in the slums, such as by providing health and sanitation programs, and campaigned against the sweatshop system and many of the other causes of poverty in the slums. Addams was in essence responsible for ushering in a national movement for enlightened and drastically needed social welfare policies.

Florence Kelley, who often worked with Jane Addams, could be called the mother of the consumer protection movement that thrives to this day. Kelley was executive secretary of the National Consumers League for thirty-two years and not only demanded and got consumer protection laws but also worked feverishly through educational campaigns and boycotts against the exploitation of workers, particularly working children. Children as young as six were toiling in canneries, mines, and airless mills. They were frequently injured or killed on the job. And they were grossly underpaid. In the sewing sweatshops, for example, they made only about four cents an hour. The League's pioneering efforts eventually resulted in the Fair Labor Standards Act of 1938, which abolished child labor.

Margaret Sanger—a public-health nurse whose mother bore

eleven children and died at age forty-eight—led a decades-long fight to abolish laws that made it illegal for doctors to distribute birth control devices or even information on how women could limit the number of children they had. Sanger believed that being forced to bear numerous children seriously undermined a woman's health and was a major contributing factor to poverty. In defiance of the law, Sanger opened the first birth control clinic in the United States in 1916. The clinic was located in a poor section of Brooklyn, and more than 150 women waited in line the day it opened. Later, a sweatshop worker who already had eight children would plead, "If you don't help me, I'll chop up a glass and swallow it tonight!" Police arrested Sanger and shut down the clinic on its tenth day of operation. Though Sanger encountered strong opposition year after year—and was jailed at least nine times for her efforts—she lived to see the dispensing of birth control legalized in the United States in 1937.

Women also sparked reform by introducing readers to the horrible lives of various downtrodden Americans through fiction. Harriet Beecher Stowe's *Uncle Tom's Cabin*, for example, roused into action northerners who had been indifferent about slavery (see #18). Elizabeth S. Phelps Ward's 1871 *The Silent Partner* detailed inhumane factory conditions. *Ramona*, authored by Helen Hunt Jackson and published in 1884, was an impassioned account of the plight of American Indians and a plea for justice.

#25. *Females actually behave much better than males when it comes to truly frightening situations.*

This one should neatly quash any taunt along the lines of "Girls are such scaredy-cats!" True, girls are more likely than boys to scream or run when they see a mouse or spider, mainly because people don't admonish or make fun of girls for showing fear as they do boys. But when it comes to the truly big scary stuff—such as an earthquake or a tornado—women are much better able than men to cope and function. Many studies support this, including an important one conducted during World War II that showed that in the heavily bombed residential areas of London and Kent, 70 percent more men than women broke down and needed psychiatric help. Another source says that under blockade, bombardment, and concentration camp conditions during the two World Wars, more men were psychiatric casualties at a ratio of seventy to one. As author/editor/publisher Leonard Woolf (Virginia's husband) once observed, "With or without screaming, women in dangerous situations are more apt to turn and do something, while men seem to lapse into a catatonic state."

Females not only cope better with *emotional* pain . . .

#26. Doctors agree that females bear physical pain far better than males do.

This is pretty impressive when you consider that because females are more "tactilely sensitive" than males we feel pain more acutely than they do.

Why are females better at enduring pain? The theory: It's Mother Nature's way of preparing us for labor and delivery.

At any rate, as Theo Lang put it in *The Difference Between a Man and a Woman*, "The exhortation commonly addressed to an injured weeping boy 'Be a man!' might be better phrased 'Be a woman!'"

#27. *Females instituted early-childhood education in America.*

While visiting Germany in 1871, Susan Blow of St. Louis became acquainted with and enamored of the kindergarten program designed by the late German educator Friedrich Froebel. Froebel had coined the term "kindergarten"—which translates as children's garden—to convey the impression that in this type of class young children could grow freely like plants in a garden as they participated in a set routine of organized games, songs, and stories, plus gardening and other constructive work.

An enthusiastic Blow returned to St. Louis and convinced William T. Harris, then superintendent of the city's schools, to let her introduce kindergarten into the school system. To prepare herself for the task, Blow went to New York City in 1872 to further study kindergarten methods with Maria Kraus-Boelte, a student of Froebel's widow. When Blow returned to St. Louis in 1873, she opened the first public-school kindergarten in America at the Des Peres School. (The first *private* kindergarten in America had been established years earlier—in 1855—in Wisconsin. But it, too, was founded by a woman, Mrs. Carl Schurz.)

In 1874 Blow opened a training school for kindergarten teachers and saw her innovation take off in popularity. By 1880, kindergartens had become fixtures throughout the St. Louis school system, and the concept was spreading across the United States. By the turn of the century, the United States counted 225,394 kindergartners (58 percent of whom attended kindergarten in public schools).

In the 1920s and 1930s, more and more American women entered the labor market so that nursery schools, which seized upon and simplified many of the kindergarten methods for use with three- and four-year-olds, also increased in popularity. The first nursery school in America had also been founded by a woman, Joanna Bethune. A teacher who had done extensive charity work among the poor in New York City, Bethune founded the Infant School Society in 1827 and a few months later opened the first "infant school," designed for children age eighteen months to five years. She intended the school to provide a little child-care relief for working-class parents. Soon Bethune was supervising nine such schools throughout New York City, and another early-childhood education innovation was spreading across America.

Incidentally, historians and educators credit yet another woman—Dr. Maria Montessori—with having had enormous influence on the evolution of the nursery school over the years. Montessori, an Italian physician and teacher, did not like the way traditional European classes were so dominated by the teacher; children had little opportunity to learn on their own. So she devised games, methods, and materials to encourage children between two and five to do it themselves— be it vocabulary building or motor-skill development—while the teacher remained in the background. Her books, including *The Montessori Method* (1912), have been widely read by teachers for generations.

And we cannot leave a discussion about the spectacular achievements of women in early-childhood education without mentioning Joan Ganz Cooney, who in 1969 created a place called Sesame Street. Cooney, who had been producing public television documentaries in New York City, was a pioneer in tapping television as an educational resource for kids. "If this country can get a man on the moon," she said in those days, "surely we should be able to figure out how to use this instrument for the betterment of society." She had become aware that while children from middle-class homes arrived on the first day of kindergarten already knowing their numbers and letters, disadvantaged kids didn't. She designed "Sesame Street" to bring these poorer kids up to par through humor, music, and great graphics. But middle-class kids also fell in love with the program (which is aired on PBS), and that doesn't bother Cooney one bit. "It was always meant to help all kids," she said in an interview with *Changing Times* magazine on the occasion of the show's twentieth anniversary. "But the disadvantaged kids were the bull's-eye of the target."

Has "Sesame Street" done its job? There's been some argument about this over the years. The program's been accused, for example, of achieving little more than "rote memorization" and of teaching children "to read not books but television." But a number of studies carried out since the early 1970s have consistently shown that all kids who watch the show have a marked improvement in cognizant skills over those who don't. And so many millions of kids watch it that, shortly after "Sesame Street" went on the air, the kindergarten curriculum had to be upgraded. Said child and adolescent psychiatrist David Fassler in a recent issue of *Healthy Kids*: "Kids come to preschool and first grade with a much more developed sense of knowledge, which they appear to have acquired through 'Sesame Street.' "

So long live Big Bird, Bert, Ernie, Prairie Dawn . . . and their mom.

P.S. "Barney," another hugely popular PBS program for kids—starring a dinosaur who's been called "the Elvis for toddlers"—was also created by women: Sheryl Leach and Kathy Parker.

#28. *Females hear better than males.*

*E*specially in the higher ranges—high as in soprano—of sound. We're more sensitive to *louder* sounds, too. When a noise is 85 decibels or above, it sounds twice as loud to us as it does to males, which explains why they can crank the stereo up to 8 and still do their homework. Ironically, however, most females can tolerate much more noise and show fewer ill effects than males can, according to Dr. Joyce Brothers. We're also better at noticing small changes in volume, which explains "women's superior sensitivity to that 'tone of voice' which their male partners are so often accused of adopting," say geneticist Anne Moir and writer David Jessel in their book *Brain Sex: The Real Difference Between Men and Women.* And we have better auditory memory—that is, we are better at remembering what we hear. Some experts believe that's why so many more females than males can sing in tune (see #15).

We have better hearing, say Moir and Jessel, because the female brain is organized to respond more sensitively to all sensory stimuli, and that includes not just sound, but taste, touch, and smell as well.

#29. A female won more medals and tournaments and set more records in more sports than any other athlete—male or female—in this century.

She was Mildred "Babe" Didrikson Zaharias, she lived from 1914 to 1956, and she was a superstar in every sport she competed in. Nicknamed "Babe" because people believed her ability was on a par with Babe Ruth, she first gained attention as a basketball star at her Texas high school, then spent two years on the nationally famous women's basketball team of the Employers Casualty Company in Dallas. Meanwhile, she was also breaking track and field records and winning swimming and figure-skating medals. In the 1932 Olympics, she won gold medals in the 80-meter hurdle and the javelin. Didrikson broke the world record in the 80-meter hurdle, then broke the javelin record by 14 feet and would have done even better than that had her hand not slipped on the javelin.

On that same Olympic trip, she tried golf for the first time, won her first game (against three sports reporters), and became passionate about the sport. Didrikson won the USA National Women's Championship by the biggest margin ever in 1946 and went on to take seventeen straight golf titles in 1947. Despite the fact that she had cancer surgery in 1953, Zaharias won the U.S. Women's Open in 1954.

She excelled at every sport she ever tried—and there are more. She set the women's record for throwing a baseball (296 feet), was one of the best field place kickers in the United States, trained as a boxer, was a top-notch diver and lacrosse player, and toured with the National Exhibition Billiards Team.

Incidentally, Zaharias's skills weren't limited to the playing field. The phenomenal Babe was a featured harmonica soloist on a Texas radio station at the age of seven, and she also sang and played harmonica in vaudeville shows as an adult.

BONUS!

Females walk faster than males.

The average woman walks 256 feet per minute while the average man does 245, according to the *Harper's Index Book.*

#30. *Females have more empathy for others than males do.*

*E*mpathy is understanding how another person feels . . . and being moved by that person's feelings. Numerous studies—one source counts sixteen—have shown females to be more empathetic than males. In one famous study, participants were asked to administer an electric shock to someone who was learning a task every time that person made a mistake. Females administered milder shocks than males . . . and this difference became even more pronounced if the female shocker had been introduced to the shockee before the experiment began.

Other studies have shown that small girls are more likely than small boys to comfort or help their mothers when they seem distressed, and to offer help, sympathy, comfort, and their own toys to distressed children.

Some experts insist that empathy is a *learned* behavior in females, not a biological imperative. They point to studies that show that when little girls do something wrong, their parents encourage them to think about how their actions affect others while little boys are simply punished and told to stop it. Psychiatrist Joan Shapiro believes males have difficulty empathizing because they are taught from a young age to suppress their own feelings—"Big boys don't cry," for example. Psychotherapist Lillian Rubin feels that boys teach *themselves* not to feel. Rubin says in her book *Just Friends* that when a boy is very young he must stop identifying with his mother and start identifying with his father in order to establish his identity as a male. "To protect against the pain wrought by the radical shift in his internal world, the child builds a set of defenses that will serve him, for good or for ill, for the rest of his life," Rubin says. She adds that one of these defenses serves as a barrier between the boy and his feelings. The bottom line, in any case: How are they supposed to understand feelings in others, Shapiro asks in her book *Men*, when they don't have the feelings themselves?

Nevertheless, if empathy is a product of nurture instead of nature, how do we account for the well-documented fact that newborn baby girls—much more often than newborn boys—cry as if in sympathy when they hear other babies cry?

BONUS!

People of both sexes smile more at females than at males.

One possible explanation: The females they're smiling at were probably already smiling. Females smile more than males do, according to numerous studies.

#31. It was a female who first exposed the harm humans were doing to the environment, igniting the world's environmental movement.

*I*n the late 1950s, an eminent marine biologist named Rachel Carson began to collect facts about what pesticides were *really* doing. Instead of just killing bugs on plants, as these chemicals were intended, they were also poisoning the plants themselves, the air, the water, and the land, and killing birds, fish . . . and probably humans as well. "These chemicals are now stored in the bodies of the vast majority of human beings, regardless of age," Carson wrote. (Decades later, in 1993, a female chemist—Mary S. Wolff—would release a study showing that women with the highest exposure to DDT, one of the most popular and deadly pesticides, had four times the breast-cancer risk of woman with the least exposure.)

In 1962 Carson published her warnings and the facts that supported them in a book called *Silent Spring,* a title she chose because she feared that if indiscriminate use of toxic chemicals continued, we'd never again hear birds sing because all of them would be dead.

The book, which became an instant best-seller, alarmed

the public. People joined in a grass-roots campaign to put an end to reckless pesticide use. Legislation was passed to ban the use of DDT. And magazines like *Time* and *Newsweek* began to regularly cover environmental damage—and not just from pesticides—that was occurring all over the world.

Carson died of cancer in 1964. She did not live to see just how big the environmental revolution she had started would become. In 1970, for example, the United States would create the federal Environmental Protection Agency. And on April 22 of that year millions of Americans would demonstrate against pollution to mark the very first Earth Day. But Rachel Carson died happy. "I had said I could never again listen happily to a thrush song if I had not done all I could," she had written to a friend. "And last night the thoughts of all the birds and other creatures and all the loveliness that is in nature came to me with such a surge of deep happiness, now that I had done what I could."

#32. Females commit far, far fewer crimes than males.

Almost eight times as many males as females were arrested for violent crimes—murder, rape, robbery, and aggravated assault—in the United States in 1991, the latest year for which statistics are available. Even when you count up the arrests for all crimes in 1991—including relatively minor offenses like forging a check or spray painting graffiti on a freeway sign—you'll find four and a half times more males than females. That same year, 90.7 percent of inmates in local jails throughout America were males; only 9.3 percent were females. And this isn't just an American phenomenon. A recent survey of arrests for all crimes in twenty-five different countries revealed that males are five to fifty times more likely to be arrested than females.

Why is crime such a male province? Researchers believe the answer has both biological and environmental components. Males are born with a greater potential for violence because they have far more testosterone, the hormone that has proved to be the source of aggressive behavior. According to Columbia University's Myriam Miedzian, higher levels of testosterone create a lower threshold for frustration, more irritability and impatience, greater impulsiveness, a tendency to rough and tumble, and perhaps a greater concern with dominance, "all of which," she says in her book *Boys Will Be Boys*, "can easily be precursors of violence."

But testosterone alone does not breed violent males, according to Miedzian and other experts. It's society that does that. As anthropologist Ashley Montagu said in Phil Donahue's book *The Human Animal*, "Every human being comes into this world loving and trustful and devoid of violent aggression. A violent society like ours creates violent people by warping its children with lessons in violence. Children in societies have their love and trust crippled or destroyed by the institutionalized, approved role models for males that teach them to be aggressive, competitive, and violent. . . ." like the Terminator.

So role models are one thing. Other research has suggested that the root of most violent crime may be the tendency of males to deny it when they are depressed (just as they suppress *most* feelings—see #30) and to not seek treatment for that condition. In *Boys Will Be Boys*, Miedzian also points to the fact that boys are much more likely to have certain physical disabilities—such as Attention Deficit Disorder with Hyperactivity (ADDH)—that put them at greater risk for behaving violently.

Finally worth noting is the theory—corroborated by several studies and sources—that violence in men can be linked to the fact that they don't give birth to children nor have they traditionally taken a major role in rearing them. The now-retired Rutgers University psychologist Dorothy Dinnerstein, like the eminent anthropologist Margaret Mead, believes that men suffer from "womb envy"—frustration at being unable to give birth to children. As a result, men feel that if their contribution to the world can't be to *create* someone, it will be to *do* something. That plus the male's innate aggressiveness has led to a lot of constructive achievements, says Dinnerstein . . . but it can go the other way, as well. "If you don't have the sense of efficacy that comes from helping another human being," she said in *The Human Animal*, "making it possible for another human being to become human, to join the human condition, to change from a helpless infant into a competent child—if you don't have that power" you're more likely to want to go out and impose your will on other people—to hurt, rape, or even kill them. Miedzian explains it another way: To raise a child, she says, one must learn considerable patience, nurturance, and empathy—and when qualities like those increase, studies have shown that violence decreases.

#33. Females make terrific bosses.

*I*n the last few years, researchers have uncovered some key differences in the way women lead others compared to the way men do. Because of the higher value we place on interpersonal relationships—and our greater success with such relationships (see #38)—women are likelier to use a more open and interactive style of management. That is, we talk more frankly with our subordinates, share information and power with them, encourage their input, make ourselves more accessible to them (by leaving our office doors open almost all the time, for example), and enhance their self-worth. Men's traditional style of management, in contrast, is more authoritarian and militaristic—there's a rigid chain of command, lots of rules and regulations, and a greater reliance on the use of rewards and punishments to accomplish goals.

Anne Moir and David Jessel, authors of *Brain Sex*, feel another female attribute that's a golden asset in management is what they call our "emotional X-ray vision"—also known as women's intuition (see #7). In clinching a business deal or participating in labor negotiations, they suggest, we have the ability to pick up discreet cues from the demeanor and tone of voice of the other side.

Finally, says Sally Helgesen, in her book *The Female Advantage: Women's Ways of Leadership,* women who are mothers are especially well equipped for management, because being a boss demands many of the same skills: "organization, pacing, the balancing of conflicting claims, teaching, guiding, leading, monitoring, handling disturbances, imparting information." Helgesen quotes one of the many female managers she interviewed: "If you can figure out which one gets the gumdrop, the four-year-old or the six-year-old, you can negotiate any contract in the world."

The labor force is changing, and in the coming years new workers will be mostly women and minorities. In fact, it's estimated that by the year 2000 women will fill two out of every three new jobs. This reality, according to *Time* magazine, ensures that "the emerging female style of management will become more prevalent, not only because more women will achieve positions of power but also because a flexible, mediating approach will be vital in dealing with America's ever more heterogeneous workers."

BONUS!

Children learn tasks better when led by female models rather than by male models.

This was proved in a test of six- and seven-year-olds, and held true even when the task was building with blocks, which is traditionally viewed as a male activity.

#34. Females made the two greatest discoveries of our time in genetics—the study of what makes each living thing unique.

Genetic scientist Barbara McClintock spent decades alone in a field on Long Island, New York, studying Indian corn as it grew. In the late 1940s, as a result of her observations, she proposed a theory that set prevailing scientific theory on its ear: Inherited characteristics are *not* logical and predictable, she said. To put it more technically, McClintock asserted that genes—the units on chromosomes by which hereditary characteristics are transmitted and determined—aren't fixed on the chromosomes in permanent locations. Instead, they can jump from one position to another in unpredictable ways. This discovery explains how an organism can adapt and change in future generations; it's how bacteria can become resistant to antibiotics, for example, and how once-normal cells turn into cancer cells.

Unfortunately, the scientific community scoffed at McClintock's finding for years. But that didn't faze her. "If you know you are on the right track, if you have this inner knowledge, then nobody can turn you off," she said in Allen L. Hammond's book *A Passion to Know.* And she was eventually vindicated. In 1983, when she was eighty-one, McClintock was awarded the Nobel Prize for medicine. The Nobel Committee called McClintock's "jumping genes" theory "one of the two great discoveries of our time in genetics."

And the other great discovery, according to the committee? It was when scientists determined the structure of DNA, the acid in each cell responsible for telling the cell—and ultimately the entire organism or individual—what to look like. Credit for this is traditionally given to James Watson, Francis Crick, and Maurice Wilkins (they won a Nobel Prize in 1962) . . . but they could not have done it without biophysicist Rosalind Franklin. Wilkins was Franklin's supervisor in a research lab at London's Kings College, and it was there that she managed to get the first successful X-ray diffraction picture of the DNA molecule. Wilkins showed this to his friends Watson and Crick, who were stalled in their own research. Using Franklin's photo and some of their own calculations and findings, they went on to build the first DNA model. Why didn't Franklin get any credit for her crucial role in all this? Only the fact that she didn't get in on the Nobel can be satisfactorily explained: Nobel Prizes are awarded only to *living* persons, and Franklin died of cancer—bitter about her lack of recognition—in 1958 at the age of thirty-seven.

A woman was responsible for still another enormously important genetic discovery. In 1905, biologist and geneticist

Nettie Stevens, who had been studying a certain kind of beetle, was the first to demonstrate that sex is determined by a particular chromosome. She identified the X and Y chromosomes and showed that the XX combination produces a female and the XY a male. Before that, scientists had believed that external factors like the temperature and what food was eaten determined the sex of offspring of the lower forms of life, like the beetle, and that divine intervention determined it in humans.

Unfortunately, this is another discovery for which a male scientist—Edmund B. Wilson—traditionally gets the credit. He was conducting similar research at the same time Stevens was and published his findings during the same year. Interestingly, however, in his initial report he said that his findings were "in agreement with the observations of Stevens," which seems to prove that she made the discovery first. In addition, according to the authors of *Mothers of Invention,* Wilson "couldn't or wouldn't be as specific as Stevens in defining these actual X and Y chromosomes" in that first paper, though a few years later—after Stevens died of cancer in 1912—he duplicated and confirmed her findings.

#35. *Females get fewer viral and bacterial illnesses than males do.*

We're not only less susceptible to the major diseases (see #16), we get fewer colds, flus, strep throats, and other such bugs. We're simply better at producing the antibodies that fight these invading viruses and bacteria. Why? Researchers suspect it's because we have two X chromosomes in our genetic makeup, while males have one X and one Y, and it's the X that carries many of the genes that control immunity. In essence, we have double protection. If something goes wrong with our first X, our bodies can turn to the second for help in fighting infections. Males have no such recourse. For this same reason males are overwhelmingly more likely to be born with conditions like hemophilia and color blindness. These conditions are carried on the X chromosome and in women are almost always counteracted by the other X.

BONUS!

Fewer females than males get acne.

It's because males have more testosterone, the hormone that stimulates the sebaceous gland to produce more of the oil that clogs pores and leads to pimples.

And hey, we can much more easily camouflage the zits we do get. With makeup, of course. While makeup on men has become acceptable in a couple of career fields in a couple of big cities, the vast majority of men consider it strictly off-limits to them.

Yes, a man can grow a beard to hide a broken-out chin, but such an addition is hot and scratchy, cannot simply be washed off at the end of the day, and must be checked frequently during meals for the presence of grody food particles. Nor will a beard cover a pimply nose or forehead.

#30. A female founded the largest organization in the United States.

She was Dr. Ethel Percy Andrus, and it's the American Association of Retired Persons (AARP), which has 32 million members. An incredible 52 percent of all Americans age fifty and older belong to AARP; 6,000 to 8,000 people join the organization *every day.*

The AARP began as the National Retired Teachers Association (NRTA) in 1947. Andrus, a retired high school principal, founded the NRTA because she was a crusader. As the leader of the NRTA, she fought in the California state legislature for pension reform for retired teachers and in the U.S. Congress for tax benefits for them. Soon she turned her attention to the greatest fear of retirees at that time: What would happen to them if they sustained a major injury or became gravely ill and required lengthy hospitalization? The problem: In those days, no insurance company would provide health insurance for a person older than sixty-five.

Eventually Andrus, with the help of others, convinced an insurance company to cover her group. This was considered a real breakthrough, and the NRTA began to receive thousands of letters from retired people who *weren't* teachers but who wanted in on the insurance, too. And that's why the NRTA evolved into the AARP.

Today the AARP's goal is to improve every aspect of life for older people. With its enormous membership muscle, the group does this through legislative lobbying, research, and education. Besides offering its members several forms of insurance, the AARP runs a mail-order and walk-in pharmacy service that fills some 7.5 million prescriptions per year and publishes *Modern Maturity*, which, with its 22.5 million subscribers, has surpassed *TV Guide* to become the magazine with the largest circulation in the United States.

#37. *Females are more flexible and limber than males.*

*T*hanks to estrogen, our joints and muscles are looser, and thanks to our greater production of the hormone called relaxin, our ligaments, which tie muscles to bones, are softer and stretchier. For these reasons, we are more flexible than males, an advantage that prompted Long Island surgeon Elizabeth Coryllos to once remark in *Ms.* magazine, "The female is essentially a thoroughbred; the male is a quarter horse."

We retain this edge throughout life. A widely quoted statistic: At age sixty, women have 90 percent of both the strength and the flexibility they had at age twenty; sixty-year-old men have only 60 percent.

Social biologist K. F. Dyer of the University of Adelaide in Australia wrote in his book *Challenging the Men* that our greater flexibility gives us "longer running strides, better hurdling techniques, and better kick and arm movements in swimming than would be expected on simple comparisons with men of the same height and weight."

#38. *The friendships between females are richer, deeper, stronger, more intimate, and more affectionate than those between males.*

Researchers have confirmed that this is true—beginning in childhood and continuing through adolescence and into adulthood—in study after study. As a male writer once lamented in a *Newsweek* essay, "In our society, it seems as if you've got to have a bosom to be a buddy." What accounts for our higher-quality friendships? One reason, according to Letty Cottin Pogrebin, author of the book *Among Friends*, is that in our society females are much more free to touch other females than males are to touch other males. And since touching—such as by giving a hug—is the primary way to show affection, males don't show much affection to their male friends.

Second, in conversation with their friends, females talk about much more intimate subjects than males do with their male friends, and this shared intimacy promotes closeness. According to Pogrebin, women communicate with their best friends on three levels: topical (politics, work, events), relational (the friendship itself), and personal (one's thoughts and feelings). Men, on the other hand, stick to topical subjects.

Why? Because men do not want to reveal their weaknesses to other men. "Men are supposed to be functional, to spend their time working or otherwise solving or thinking about how to solve problems," explains attorney Marc Feigen Fasteau, author of *The Male Machine*. "Personal reaction, how one feels about something, is considered dysfunctional, at best an irrelevant distraction from the expected objectivity." When psychotherapist Lillian B. Rubin, who wrote the book *Just Friends*, did a study on the differences between male and female friendships, one of her male participants explained this inability to show vulnerability by saying, "I think men are afraid of each other. It's like we've been trained to be on guard."

On guard and *competitive*, says Fasteau. Competitiveness is the principal way men relate to each other, he says, first because they don't know how else to make contact and second because competitiveness is the perfect way to exhibit those key masculine traits like toughness and ability to dominate. But this competitiveness, says Fasteau, is a barrier to openness between men.

Rubin says that when men have personal problems they *will* attempt to discuss them with male friends, but that what usually happens is "an abstract discussion, held under cover of an intellectual search for understanding rather than a revelation" of their lives and feelings. If a man is worried about the constant fights he's having with his wife, for example, he's more likely to launch a discussion of, say, the difficulty of communicating with women in general than to get specific about his own situation. Fasteau agrees: "Everything is discussed as though it were taking place out there somewhere, as though we had no more felt response to it than to the weather."

Another difference between female and male friendships: Both Pogrebin and Rubin say females *nurture* their friends and provide emotional support, but males don't. In other words, if a female suddenly has a crisis—say she gets fired—her female friends will rush to offer comfort and support. Most males don't do this for their male friends because they consider nurturing to be *female* behavior.

Finally, the friendships of females are deeper and more meaningful than those of males because they are what Pogrebin calls more "holistic." That is, female friends tend to do everything together, while males tend to have different friends for different activities. For example, a man might have one friend to jog with, another for discussing work concerns, and a third for attending sports events. The roles of these friends rarely overlap. A female, on the other hand, most likely does all of these things with the same person or persons.

What does a male lose because of these restrictions on his friendships? ". . . The experience of knowing another person fully and completely and of *being* known himself," concludes Pogrebin. And what do females gain? Say Caryl Rivers, Rosalind Barnett, and Grace Baruch, who wrote the book *Beyond*

Sugar and Spice: How Women Grow, Learn, and Thrive: "The friendships and the capacity for intimacy that girls develop while growing up may serve them in later years as a bulwark against loneliness, failure, and feelings of alienation. And these resources may be one of the great contributions of female socialization. Women in later life often find that this capacity for intimacy, which may have begun in the games of childhood, is a sustaining, life-giving force."

#39. *Females ushered in the nuclear age.*

*I*n Paris in the waning years of the nineteenth century, scientist Marie Curie coined the term "radioactivity" for the rays of energy that were spontaneously emitted from the elements uranium and thorium. She and her husband, Pierre, then went on to discover two new elements that were also radioactive—polonium, which Marie named after her native Poland, and radium, which they found to be 2 million times more radioactive than uranium. This work earned them a Nobel Prize in physics in 1903; Marie went on to win another Nobel Prize in chemistry in 1911 for isolating radium in its pure state (making her the only person ever to win two Nobels—and what makes that even more spectacular is that she got them in different disciplines).

Since then, radium has become an almost miraculous weapon against cancer, and Curie's discovery of the element is what she is usually noted for in the history books. But, according to Rosalynd Pflaum, author of a Madame Curie biography called *Grand Obsession*, she made an even more important contribution: Madame Curie was the first to hypothesize that the atoms of radioactive material might yield immense energy . . . and that was the start of the nuclear age.

Marie's daughter, Irène Joliot-Curie, carried on her mother's work and in 1935 won her own Nobel in chemistry in conjunction with her husband Frédéric Joliot-Curie. They had discovered that it's possible to make certain nonradioactive elements—like aluminum and magnesium—artificially radioactive. This was not only a vital step toward releasing the energy of the atom, it also, like Marie's discovery, had immense therapeutic value. Today injections of Irène and Frédéric's artificially created radioisotopes, as they're called, are frequently used to treat leukemia.

Another scientist working in the field pioneered by Marie Curie, German physicist Lise Meitner, was the first to split the nucleus of a uranium atom (an atom being a basic part of a molecule, which is, in turn, a basic building block of all matter). She called this splitting of an atom "nuclear fission."

Meitner, who first became interested in atomic physics when as a student she read newspaper stories about the Curie discovery of radium, was also the first scientist to calculate and report just how much energy potential nuclear fission had. As she wrote in an article in 1939, "It seems therefore possible that the uranium nucleus has only small stability of form and may, after neutron capture, divide itself into two nuclei of roughly equal size. These two nuclei will repel each other (because they both carry large positive charges) and should gain a total kinetic energy of about 200 million electron volts." That happens to be 20 million times more energy than an equal amount of TNT.

Later she would say that "we were unaware what kind of powerful genie we were releasing from a bottle." This was because, unfortunately, she made her discovery on the eve of World War II, and scientists in several countries immediately sought to turn this new source of energy into a weapon—a turn of events that Meitner adamantly opposed. Though she was invited to join the scientists who were at work on the weapon, she refused (in fact, the horrified Meitner stopped working on nuclear fission *period*). "I myself have not worked on smashing the atom with the idea of producing death-dealing weapons," she said. "You must not blame us scientists for the use to which war technicians put our discoveries." What those war technicians built was the atomic bomb that very nearly annihilated the entire Japanese city of Hiroshima in 1945.

Meitner's discovery, however, was life *saving*, as well. It was essential to the continuing development of nuclear medicine, which the Curies' work had begun. And it's thanks to Meitner—who Albert Einstein once called "the German Marie Curie"—that we now have in these days of energy consciousness and dwindling natural resources a new source of electricity: the nuclear reactor.

BONUS!

Females snore less than males.

About one in four adults snores, but more of those snorers are males than females. Incidentally, researchers have measured snores as loud as 69 decibels, which is roughly as earsplitting as standing ten feet from a jackhammer.

#40. Females have much greater freedom in what we can wear.

When your daughter opens her closet each morning, she probably faces a dizzying array of selections. Weather permitting, she can choose to wear a long dress or skirt, a short dress or skirt, a split skirt, overalls, jumpsuit, leggings, jeans, pants, sweater, blouse, T-shirt, vest, bodysuit, and on and on. In the past few years, it's even been perfectly acceptable—if not the height of fashion—for a female to appear in public wearing a tuxedo, a tie, a man's shirt, or even his boxer shorts. Males, on the other hand, have only a fraction of the choices when it comes to attire.

Females haven't always been so lucky. In the eighteenth and nineteenth centuries, women were required to wear long, hooped, ground-sweeping skirts for modesty's sake, and were expected to have slender waists, which they played up or faked by wearing numerous hot, itchy, scratchy petticoats under their skirts and by cinching their waists six or seven inches smaller with the help of a torturous corset reinforced with whalebone. And that was it. You had to dress like that no matter how bad the weather, how muddy the streets, or how physical your labor. (Remember Scarlett O'Hara out in the field in that "as God is my witness" turnip-eating scene?)

The winds of change began to blow in the early 1850s when Elizabeth Smith Miller, who loved to garden, designed an outfit to make it easier to do that. The outfit consisted of Turkish pantaloons partially covered by a belted tunic and a skirt that fell four inches below the knee (a *scandalous* length!). Miller wore it while visiting her cousin, feminist Elizabeth Cady Stanton (see #22) and Stanton's friend Amelia Bloomer, who in 1849 founded America's first women's rights newpaper, the *Lily*. Bloomer loved the outfit and promoted it in the *Lily* as part of her crusade for dress reform, which she felt was essential since hoop skirts had gotten so ridiculously wide that it was hard for women to go through doorways. When other American newpapers also began to publish pictures and stories about the costume, they mistakenly credited Bloomer with the design, which explains why that style of trousers became known as bloomers instead of millers. Soon bloomers were more fiercely debated than slavery across the United States.

While bloomers were undoubtedly more practical and comfortable than what was then fashionable, they did not last. It seems that women who wore them—including Susan B. Anthony and Elizabeth Cady Stanton—were literally laughed off the street, had rocks thrown at them by angry males, and were ejected from public establishments. By 1853 even the bravest souls gave them up—except for Bloomer. She insisted on wearing them into the 1860s, and even after she, too, dropped them as street wear, she wore them while cleaning her house.

It would be another 100 years before wearing trousers became acceptable for women. Even so, Bloomer's campaign sent hoopskirts—at long last—on their way out of fashion, and more practical attire for women became available. Bloomer died in December 1894, campaigning against alcohol and for women's rights up to the end. "But the crusade for which she will longest be remembered," says Jules Archer in his book *The Unpopular Ones,* "is the one that eventually liberated women to move about as freely and comfortably as men—often more so—in slacks, short skirts, shorts, bikinis, and miniskirts."

#41. *Females have superior fine motor skills and manual dexterity.*

*I*n a laboratory setting, our more precise hand movements make us better than males—even when we're as young as three and a half—at tests like moving a row of small pegs from one area to another on a pegboard. Outside the laboratory— in real life—our dexterity makes us better at needlework and neurosurgery. And it gives us better handwriting. The explanation: Our muscles are controlled by two systems—the extra-pyramidal system, which controls all of our large muscles, and the pyramidal, which is in charge of fine movements. The female pyramidal system is better developed than the male. The female hormone estrogen probably plays a role in this, too, according to anthropologist Helen Fisher. She says our dexterity actually gets even better around ovulation, when our estrogen levels are at their highest.

#42. *Females made many of the biggest medical breakthroughs of the twentieth century.*

Millions of people throughout the world have been saved from untimely deaths thanks to the medical advances made by women.

Near the turn of the century, for example, during a raging diphtheria epidemic, pathologist Anna Wessel Williams developed a potent antitoxin for the disease, which was a major killer of children. Thanks to the antitoxin, which is still being produced today, diphtheria is rare in the Western world. Williams is also responsible for bringing to America the then-new rabies antitoxin, which was developed at the Pasteur Institute in Paris.

Also near the turn of the century, physician Dorothy Reed Mendenhall identified the cell that causes Hodgkin's disease, a form of cancer. Her discovery—named the Reed cell, after Mendenhall's maiden name—disproved the prevailing theory that Hodgkin's was a form of tuberculosis.

By studying the diets of puppies, researcher May Mellanby noticed how changes in those diets affected the puppies' teeth. Her studies led to the cure for rickets—a painful condition caused by softening and weakening of the bones—and other forms of vitamin D deficiency. In fact, another woman scientist—Martha May Eliot—is credited with codeveloping that cure in the 1920s: lots of sunshine and cod-liver oil, both of which are rich sources of Vitamin D. (Eliot is also credited with introducing the use of social workers in public-health programs.)

Edith Quimby, a biophysicist, gets the historical credit for developing the field of radiation therapy—that is, using X rays and radium to treat cancer and other diseases in humans. Quimby did decades of research, beginning in 1919, to make it possible to determine the exact forms and dosages of radiation required for treatment.

Medical researcher Louise Pearce was coinventor in 1919 of the serum that cures sleeping sickness—a dreaded disease that inflamed the brain, created a continual state of sleepiness, and was killing thousands of people in Africa. Largely thanks to Pearce, sleeping sickness has been completely eradicated.

In the first three decades of this century, toxicologist Alice Hamilton founded the discipline of industrial medicine and became the recognized authority in that field. The lives of thousands of workers were saved because Hamilton identified and sounded the alarm about toxic substances like lead, phosphorus, and benzol that were then common in the air of factories, mines, and other workplaces. She crusaded for protective health legislation in regard to occupational diseases.

Such laws were unheard of before her time; now they're common throughout the United States.

In 1930 the director of the esteemed Rockefeller Institute of Medical Studies in New York City called his employee, anatomist Florence Sabin, "the greatest living scientist." She was a pioneer in the study of blood, having discovered in 1919 the origin of red corpuscles, for example. Sabin was the first to trace the origin and development of the lymphatic system— one of the body's most vital networks because it carries food to every single cell. She also spent many years researching tuberculosis and syphilis, which were common killers. After retiring to her native state of Colorado in the 1940s, she immersed herself in the public-health concerns of the state, pushing the legislature to pass infectious disease control and sewage disposal laws. Colorado's Sabin Bills, as they were called, resulted in tremendous drops in the death rates from tuberculosis and syphilis in the state. Sabin is also credited with leading the movement to redirect the focus of the medical community to the maintenance of health, not just the cure of disease.

Working in Ghana in the 1930s, pediatrician Cecily D. Williams identified kwashiorkor, a severe protein deficiency disease now called protein-calorie malnutrition. Honoring her years later, the American Medical Association said, "Perhaps more than any other person in the world, this great woman is responsible for the improvement of child and maternal health in developing nations."

Bacteriologist Alice Evans found the source of a terrible disease called undulant fever, which she herself had contracted and fought for seven years. The disease, then common throughout the world, came from microorganisms living in the udders of healthy-looking cows. Evans also came up with the solution to the problem: Pasteurize all milk; that is, heat it to kill the microorganisms before shipping it out to market. (The pasteurization process was then being used mainly to retard spoilage in beer and wine.) Because of Evans's work, pasteurization of milk was mandated throughout the United States in the 1930s.

During that same decade, Hattie Alexander, a physician and bacteriologist, developed an antibody for *hemophilus influenzae* meningitis, a disease in which the membranes around the brain and spinal cord are inflamed. Within two years of Alexander's discovery, deaths from this type of meningitis—which had previously been 100 percent fatal in babies—fell by 80 percent.

Another major breakthrough in pediatric medicine in the 1930s was pathologist Ruth Darrow's research that showed how a mother with an RH-negative blood factor carrying an RH-positive fetus can develop antibodies that attack and destroy the fetus's red blood cells, ultimately killing the fetus.

Because of Darrow's research, all RH-negative mothers are now immunized against this process.

Other medical milestones from the 1930s: Pathologist and pediatrician Dorothy Hansine Anderson identified cystic fibrosis, then came up with an easy way to diagnose it. Nutritionist and biochemist Gladys Anderson Emerson, working with fellow scientist Herbert M. Evans, was the first to isolate vitamin E from wheat germ—a rich source of this vitamin, which today's researchers believe may be a potent weapon against both cancer and heart disease (in fact, a recent Harvard study showed that women who take vitamin E every day cut their risk of heart disease in half). In England, Mary Walker discovered a cure for myasthenia gravis, a disease in which the voluntary muscles feel unusually fatigued. When Walker died in 1974, her obituary in a medical journal noted that hers was "the most important British contribution to therapeutic medicine up to that time."

Pediatrician Helen Taussig was responsible for developing the operation that saves "blue babies," whose skin appears bluish because of a shortage of oxygen in the blood. This condition was a leading cause of infant death before Taussig began researching it in the 1940s and discovered that the source of the problem was a malformed pulmonary artery. Since this is the artery that brings fresh blood and oxygen from the heart to the lungs, Taussig theorized that the problem could be solved if a bypass was built from the heart to the lung. Taussig teamed up with a heart surgeon, Alfred Blalock, who did just that in 1945. The Blalock-Taussig Method, as it became known, was one of the first successful human-heart operations.

In 1948 microbiologist Elizabeth Hazen and chemist Rachel Brown discovered nystatin, the first safe antibiotic to kill fungi. Since then it's been used to cure everything from ringworm and athlete's foot to fungus growing on priceless art objects. Nystatin was considered the greatest biomedical breakthrough since penicillin had been discovered in 1928; nystatin is to fungi what penicillin is to bacteria. (Incidentally, in 1926 Brown had also discovered a pneumonia vaccine that is still used today.)

In 1952, when polio was the most dreaded disease in America, Dorothy Horstman, a physician and research scientist at Yale, made a key discovery: Contrary to then-current scientific belief, the polio virus did enter the bloodstream, not just the muscles. This information was vital to the development of the polio vaccine.

Also in 1952 an anesthesiologist, Virginia Apgar, devised a test that has saved the lives of countless newborns since. The test, called the Apgar Score, is used to determine the health of a baby right after it's born—vital moments when circulatory and respiratory problems can still be corrected.

Another woman who has saved numerous infant lives is

Mary Ellen Avery, a pediatrician and authority on the infant heart. She did much of the initial research into what causes hyaline membrane disease, a respiratory disorder that's the result of an abnormal membrane lining the lungs.

Biologist Katherine Sanford gets the credit for cloning. She was the first person, in other words, to isolate a single cell and allow it to breed identical descendants. Besides providing a rich source of plot ideas for sci-fi writers, cloning made possible the culturing of viruses, the development of vaccines, and the study of metabolic disorders, according to the authors of *Women of Science: Righting the Record.*

Chemist Dorothy Mary Crowfoot Hodgkin won the Nobel Prize for chemistry in 1964 for her work in the 1940s and 1950s in determining the structure of certain chemical compounds by a technique called X-ray diffraction. She is especially known for deciphering the structure of penicillin, which was a big help in synthesizing and producing the huge quantities needed during World War II; the structure of vitamin B-12, important in the understanding and control of anemia; and the structure of insulin, which aided scientists in understanding diabetes.

Italian neurobiologist Rita Levi-Montalcini was a codiscoverer in 1954 of a biological mechanism called nerve growth factor, which stimulates the growth of nerve cells. This discovery played a vital role in helping researchers understand the way nerves act and function, and Levi-Montalcini won a Nobel Prize in 1986 because of it. Today researchers around the world continue to study nerve growth factor because they believe it can help explain the nature of cancer, Alzheimer's disease and other maladies.

Physicist Rosalyn S. Yalow invented radioimmunoassay, the use of radioactive isotopes to measure minute concentrations of vitamins, hormones, enzymes, viruses, toxins, and drugs in body tissue. Prior to Yalow's discovery, these substances were often too minuscule to detect. She was awarded the Nobel Prize in medicine in 1977, and the Nobel Committee said her technique caused "a revolution in biological and medical research."

A fourth Nobel winner: Research scientist and pharmacology educator Gertrude Belle Elion. Back in the 1940s, Elion and her partner George Hitchings figured out how normal human cell growth differs from the growth of cancer, viruses, bacteria, and parasites. With that knowledge, Elion and Hitchings went on to develop drugs to fight cancer, herpes, gout, and other diseases, and to prevent organ rejection in kidney-transplant patients. They won the Nobel Prize in medicine in 1988 for their work.

Another trailblazer in the field of organ transplantation was zoologist Barbara Bain, who developed a technique called mixed leukocyte culture (MLC) in the early 1960s. MLC plays a crucial role in organ and bone-marrow transplants by determining donor-recipient matches.

It's also thanks to a woman that there's at least one drug, azidothymidine (commonly known as AZT) that's prolonging the lives of people with AIDS. Although AZT had been around since 1964—it was first synthesized as a potential cancer fighter and found ineffective for that purpose—it was chemist Janet Rideout who decided in the mid-1980s that it should be tested against HIV, the virus believed to cause AIDS. Another woman, virologist Martha St. Clair, performed the test and found, when she checked her microscopic slide before leaving work one day, that the compound actually was inhibiting the growth of HIV. Said St. Clair in the book *Feminine Ingenuity*: "It was a moment every researcher savors!"

Finally, Andrea Stierle, a postdoctoral fellow at Montana State University, found in 1991 that a fungus growing on a yew tree—like the tree itself—contained taxol, a seemingly miraculous substance that in one study was found to significantly reduce tumors in 30 percent of women whose ovarian cancer did not respond to other treatments. (And researchers also believe taxol may turn out to be just as effective against cancerous breast and lung tumors.) The problem with taxol has been that it costs so much to extract it from yew trees that a course of treatment can run as high as $6,000. Stierle's fungus discovery, named *Taxomyces andreanae* in her honor, may make it possible to cultivate the drug much more cheaply in a lab.

BONUS!

Females get the hiccups only one-quarter as often as males do.

No one knows why this is so, nor does anybody know why we get hiccups in the first place, since they serve no useful purpose. They don't protect the windpipe from inhaling food like the gag reflex does. They don't clear the respiratory tract like a sneeze does. They're just annoying, embarrassing, and sometimes even painful.

#43. Females aren't as sensitive to cold weather. And, ironically, we also stay cooler in the summer.

We have an extra layer of fat. It's just under the skin, and thin, but it gives us seven more pounds of fat than males have. Dr. Joyce Brothers calls it an "invisible fur coat" for us in the winter. The extra fat layer also insulates us against the heat of summer. Our relative summer comfort can also be credited to the fact that our sweat glands are much more evenly distributed over our bodies than men's are, which allows us to cool off faster.

#44. *Females have a better sense of taste.*

More sensitive, more discerning. Which explains why, now that we are being given opportunities to cook in kitchens other than our own, more if not most of the world's greatest chefs will, in the future, be females.

That we have more taste only stands to reason, since we have a superior sense of smell (see #10) and these "sister senses," as they're sometimes called, are linked. When we put food in our mouths, it stimulates the taste buds on our tongues, and small particles float into the nasal cavity to stimulate the organs of smell. The brain registers all of these nerve impulses from nose and mouth as a single sensation. This is why if your nose is stuffed up and you can't smell something, you can't taste it very well either.

The advantages of superior tasting ability? Besides giving us more gastronomical pleasure, our heightened sense of taste makes us better at detecting whether or not a food might be spoiled or poisonous. Scientists speculate that evolution awarded us with great taste—our fourth superior sense (along with touch, hearing, and smell)—because heightened senses were once essential for protecting and nurturing infants. There seems to be an estrogen link, since when levels of that hormone plummet after menopause, many women report a decline in taste sensitivity. When England's Queen Victoria (see #11) was fifty-seven, for example, she complained that strawberries didn't taste as sweet as they had when she was a little girl.

The tasting ability of both females and males declines as we age for another reason—we lose taste buds. Throughout our lives, taste buds wear out, die, and are replaced within about a two-week span. But they're not replaced as frequently once we hit forty-five. A baby has far, far more taste buds than an adult (the kid even has some on the insides of her cheeks!), which may explain why most children don't count broccoli among their favorite foods.

#45. *Females don't have to shave their faces.*

Males aren't forced to either—but most of them (the adult ones, that is) feel obligated to shave, and that commitment uses up an incredible 139 days (or 3,350 hours) of a man's lifetime. Those statistics, supplied by the Gillette Company, are based on the average man who's between fifteen and seventy-five years old and who shaves about three minutes a day five days a week.

Female faces haven't always been so razor free, by the way. In the fourteenth and fifteenth centuries—as a look at Leonardo da Vinci's *Mona Lisa* will attest—women weren't considered fashionable unless they shaved off both their eyebrows plus an inch or two of hairline, resulting in a decidedly egghead effect. Later, in the sixteenth and seventeenth centuries, a permanently "surprised" look was all the rage, and since most women didn't have the eyebrows to carry it off, they shaved their real ones and substituted false ones, often made of mouse fur.

While we're on the subject of hair . . .

#40. *Females rarely go bald.*

*I*t's ironic that while males deal daily with hair where they don't want it, they usually have less hair where they *do* want it—on their heads. Both males and females shed about 100 hairs a day. But while most of ours grow back, many males lose those hairs permanently, thanks to the activity of testosterone and a common inherited nuisance called male pattern baldness. A whopping 60 percent of all adult men in America are partially or completely bald. Yes, women *can* go bald, but that's rare, and it's usually the result of a disorder of the hair follicles, not heredity.

Incidentally, another advantage we have in the hair department is that our hair grows faster than that of males. So we recover more quickly from a bad haircut. Female hair grows faster at every age and fastest of all—up to seven inches in a single year—when we're between ages sixteen and twenty-four.

#47. *Females are responsible for the two biggest advances in computer programming.*

Lady Augusta Ada Byron Lovelace is actually given credit for *inventing* computer programming. Programming is instructing the computer in its tasks. Lovelace, daughter of the famous English poet Lord Byron (of "She walks in beauty" fame), was a recognized mathematical genius in her time, in the mid-1800s. She became an associate of inventor George Babbage, who had already designed on paper a machine called the "analytic engine," which could do complex calculations and is considered the forerunner of the digital computer. It was Lovelace who devised the punch-card programs that would tell the analytic engine what to do. In 1982, the U.S. Department of Defense named a Pentagon computer language ADA in honor of Lady Lovelace's nineteenth-century contribution to the science.

Grace Murray Hopper of the U.S. Navy was the other female computer programming pioneer. In the early 1950s, Hopper, who had a Ph.D. in mathematics from Yale and who'd had a hand in the development of the world's first electronic computer (the Navy's Mark I), invented the first computer "compiler." This was a translation program that allowed for the first automatic programming. It streamlined computer programming and changed software design forever by making the computer do a number of required, repetitive, tedious tasks automatically. Before Hopper's discovery, programmers were forced to write time-consuming instructions, called codes, every time they developed a new program, and they needed to have the equivalent of a Ph.D. in math to do it. The compiler is considered the ancestor to today's computer programs.

Hopper's compiler and some of her later work paved the way for what we today call user-friendly computer programs: programs that don't require you to know a complex computer code in order to operate them. For example, if your daughter were to write a term paper about Grace Hopper on her computer and find, to her dismay, that she had misspelled the name as "Hoppre" throughout, to correct the mistake she would need only to give the computer a simple command like "FIND HOPPRE" instead of what was necessary in the olden days, something like [*#//--##a-+//**--{++} <<aee#//*2].

"Women turn out to be very good programmers for one very good reason," Hopper said in the book *Particular Passions.* "They tend to finish up things, and men don't very often finish. After men think they've solved a problem, they want to go off and get a new one, whereas a woman will always wrap it up in a neat package and document it."

Incidentally, when Hopper finally retired from the Navy in

1986 as a rear admiral, she was eighty years old and the oldest officer on active duty in the entire U.S. military. In 1991, President George Bush awarded her the U.S. Medal of Technology. She was the first individual ever, male or female, to receive that honor.

#48. *Females will soon outperform males in several of the most strenuous sports.*

*U*ntil the early 1970s, no one disputed that men were superior at most sports. But once women began to get coaching and training that had been traditionally available only to men, our performance levels in such strenuous sports as swimming and running jumped suddenly, and much more sharply than those of men. Example: Between 1963 and 1978, the best female marathon time fell from 3:50 hours to 2:50 hours, while the male time went from 2:20 to 2:10.

Applying these rates of improvement, women should overtake men in marathon running sometime in this decade, in cycling by the year 2011, and in speed swimming by 2056. Women surpassed men in channel swimming years ago. In fact, when Gertrude Ederle became the first woman to swim across the chilly English Channel (in 1926) her time broke the record of the fastest male channel swimmer by a whopping two hours. The current world record holder is Penny Dean of California, who did it in 7 hours and 40 minutes in 1978 at the age of thirteen. Another California woman, Lynne Cox, holds the overall record for swimming the Strait of Magellan and the Bering Strait, and she's the only person who has ever swum across the Cape of Good Hope and across Siberia's frigid Lake Baikal.

Our extra fat, which better insulates us against cold water (see #43), is one reason females are superior in long-distance, open-water swimming. But we make better swimmers than males *period*. Our greater flexibility (see #37) is a big help here. And the greater amount of fat in our bodies provides us with better buoyancy and less drag, with the result that we use 20 percent less energy than males do when we swim. The higher level of fat in our thighs, especially, makes it easier for us to hold our legs horizontal in the water, a position necessary for the most efficient leg action. It has even been suggested that our breasts may also be an advantage in swimming by aiding the passage of water over the body.

#49. *Females are luckier in love.*

*F*or one thing, females experience the joy of being in love more intensely than males do. When in love, females are much more likely to report feeling "giddy and carefree," "like I'm floating on a cloud," and "like I want to run, jump, and scream." We report higher levels of euphoria than males, and more of a "general feeling of well-being." T. George Harris (founder of *Psychology Today* magazine) says in the book *A New Look at Love*: "Women's bodies are kinder to them, more generous, because in passionate love they feel more physical highs." (Though he adds that this euphoria also causes us to lose more sleep when we're in love than men do!)

Females are also at an advantage when we fall *out* of love: Females get over the breakup of a love relationship more easily than males do. Says Charles T. Hill, professor of psychology at Whittier College, in *The Opposite Sex*: "Rejected men have more difficulty coping emotionally with the breakup than women in the same situation. Men become more depressed and lonely, and they have a harder time remaining friends with their former partner after the breakup." Backing him up is a study by Harvard scientists of the relationships of 231 Boston couples. These researchers, who followed the relationships for two years, concluded that women were far more resigned at the end of a relationship and were therefore better able to "pick up the pieces" and move on. Interestingly, and contrary to popular belief, the researchers also found that it was usually the women who decided whether and when a relationship should end.

Why is breaking up so hard on men? A 1991 article in *Cosmopolitan* came up with several reasons, and we'll review just a few. According to New York City family therapist Vera Paster, most men don't monitor the quality of a relationship the way most women do. So when a woman breaks it off, it comes as a big shock to the average man. Unlike women, men tend to seal up their pain instead of dealing with it, and it's the crying, talking to friends, and working through that women do that's the true source of healing, says Paster. (It doesn't help here that males have more difficulty expressing their emotions—see #6—in the first place.) And, according to *Cosmo*, although the stereotype of the male is that he is more independent than the female, males seem to have a special susceptibility to separation and loss. As toddlers, boys have to abandon their fantasies to be just like Mommy, and around the time they start kindergarten they have to come to grips with the reality that they can't marry her. "Although part of normal development," says *Cosmo*, "these losses can be traumatic. They lead psychologists like [Sam] Osherson to suspect that vulnerability to separation and loss is virtually built in to the male condition."

BONUS!

As babies, females are less fearful and irritable than males, cry less often, smile more frequently, and are quicker to potty train.

Obviously, however, this is a bonus your daughter won't be able to appreciate until she has her own baby girl!

#50. Only females can give birth.

Babies have been *conceived* in a test tube, but so far no embryo has developed into a viable human being outside the body of a woman.

Statement #50 is a terrific way to put a positive spin on the answer to the question "Mommy, why do women change their names to their husbands' names when they get married?" or "Mommy, why is your last name different from mine and Daddy's?" You then just add that because women are the givers of birth, men have traditionally given their names as their contribution to the family.

While we're on the subject of bearing children: Venerable anthropologist Margaret Mead once speculated that perhaps the reason that in the past there weren't more standout women in some of the creative fields, such as music composition, was "the greater appeal of creating and cherishing young human beings."

And maybe that *is* it, in combination with the fact that for centuries, women were actively discouraged—if not outright prohibited—from doing anything outside the confines of bearing children and keeping house.

But it's a different world now. We are living in a time in

which females can choose to raise children, or to engage in creative, satisfying work outside the home, or to even do both—either at different times in our lives (remember, we've got an extra seven years to play with) or, with lots of help, simultaneously. The choice is ours, and even the sky is no longer the limit (just ask Sally Ride). That's why now, more than at any other time in history, it's great to be a girl, wonderful to be a woman, fantastic to be female.

Suggested Reading List

Want more in-depth information about women's accomplishments and advantages? Look for the following titles, which are loosely grouped by subject, at your local bookstore. If a particular title is unavailable for purchase, check your local library.

FOR ADULTS

Brain Sex: The Real Difference Between Men and Women, by Anne Moir and David Jessel (Carol Publishing Group, 1991).

Male and Female Realities: Understanding the Opposite Sex, by Joe Tanenbaum (Robert Erdmann Publishing, 1990).

The Opposite Sex, by Anne Campbell (Salem House Publishers, 1989).

The Human Animal, by Phil Donahue (Simon & Schuster, 1985).

What's the Difference? How Men and Women Compare, by Jane Barr Stump (William Morrow & Co., 1985).

The Natural Superiority of Women, by Ashley Montagu (Collier Books, 1974).

The First Sex, by Elizabeth Gould Davis (G. P. Putnam's Sons, 1971).

Megatrends for Women, by Patricia Aburdene and John Naisbitt (Villard Books, 1992).

Hellraisers, Heroines, and Holy Women: Women's Most Remarkable Contributions to History, by Jean F. Blashfield (B & B Publishing, 1992).

The Book of Women's Firsts: Breakthrough Achievements of Almost 1,000

American Women, by Phyllis J. Read and Bernard L. Witlieb (Random House, 1992).

Womanlist, by Marjorie P. K. Weiser and Jean S. Arbeiter (Atheneum, 1981).

Particular Passions: Talks with Women Who Have Shaped Our Times, by Lynn Gilbert and Gaylen Moore (C. N. Potter/Crown, 1981).

Leading Ladies: An Affectionate Look at American Women of the Twentieth Century, by Electra Clark (Stein and Day, 1976).

Herstory: A Woman's View of American History, by June Sochen (Alfred Publishing Co., 1974).

The Book of Women's Achievements, by Joan Macksey and Kenneth Macksey (Stein and Day, 1976).

She's Nobody's Baby: A History of American Women in the 20th Century, by Suzanne Levine and Susan Dworkin (Fireside/ Simon & Schuster, 1983).

Just Friends: The Role of Friendship in Our Lives, by Lillian B. Rubin (HarperCollins, 1986).

Among Friends: Who We Like, Why We Like Them, and What We Do with Them, by Letty Cottin Pogrebin (McGraw-Hill, 1987).

Beyond Sugar and Spice: How Women Grow, Learn, and Thrive, by Caryl Rivers, Rosalind Barnett, and Grace Baruch (G. P. Putnam's Sons, 1979).

Feminine Ingenuity: Women and Invention in America, by Anne L. Macdonald (Ballantine Books, 1992).

Mothers of Invention: From the Bra to the Bomb: Forgotten Women and Their Unforgettable Ideas, by Ethlie Ann Vane and Greg Ptacek (William Morrow & Co., 1988).

The Triumph of Discovery: Women Scientists Who Won the Nobel Prize [includes the stories of Barbara McClintock, Rosalyn Yalow, and Rita Levi-Montalcini], by Joan Dash (Julian Messner, 1991).

Women of Science: Righting the Record, by G. Kass-Simon and Patricia Farnes (Indiana University Press, 1990).

Women Pioneeers of Science, by Louis Haber (Harcourt Brace Jovanovich, 1979).

Grand Obsession: Madame Curie and Her World, by Rosalynd Pflaum (Doubleday, 1989).

Are We Winning Yet? How Women Are Changing Sports and Sports Are Changing Women, by Mariah Burton Nelson (Random House, 1991).

Anatomy of Love: The Natural History of Monogamy, Adultery, and Divorce [see especially the chapter "Why Can't a Man Be More Like a Woman?"], by Helen E. Fisher (W. W. Norton Company, 1992).

The Female Advantage: Why Women Are More Effective Leaders, by Sally Helgesen (Doubleday, 1990).

Men: A Translation for Women, by Joan Shapiro, M.D. (Dutton, 1992).

What Every Woman Should Know About Men, by Dr. Joyce Brothers (Ballantine Books, 1987).

Boys Will Be Boys, by Myriam Miedzian (Doubleday, 1991).

ESPECIALLY FOR CHILDREN

Jane Addams, by Leslie Wheeler (Silver Burdett Press, 1990); grades 4–7.

Jane Addams: Pioneer in Social Reform and Activist for World Peace, by Jacquelyn Mitchard (Gareth Stevens Children's Books, 1991); grades 5–9.

Susan B. Anthony, by Barbara Weisberg (Chelsea House Publishers, 1988); grades 7–9.

Susan B. Anthony: Pioneer in Woman's Rights, by Helen Stone Peterson (Garrard Publishing Co., 1971); grades 3–5.

The Story of Rachel Carson and the Environmental Movement, by Leila M. Foster (Children's Press, 1990); grades 3–5.

Rachel Carson, by Marty Jezer (Chelsea House Publishers, 1988); grades 7–10.

Rachel Carson: Who Loved the Sea, by Jean Lee Latham (Chelsea House Publishers, 1973, 1991); grades 3–5.

Marie Curie and the Discovery of Radium, by Ann E. Steinke (Barron's, 1987); grades 5–8.

Dorothea Dix: Hospital Founder, by Mary Malone (Chelsea Juniors, 1991); grades 2–4.

Rosa Parks: The Movement Organizes, by Kai Friese (Silver Burdett Press, 1990); grades 6–9.

Harriet and the Runaway Book: The Story of Harriet Beecher Stowe and Uncle Tom's Cabin, by Johanna Johnston (Harper & Row, 1977); grades 2–6.

Aunt Harriet's Underground Railroad in the Sky [fiction based on the story of Harriet Tubman], by Faith Ringgold (Crown, 1992); grade 2 and up.

A Picture Book of Harriet Tubman, by David A. Adler (Holiday House, 1992); grades 2–4.

Harriet Tubman: Slavery and the Underground Railroad, by Megan McClard (Silver Burdett Press, 1991); grades 6–9.

Babe Didrikson Zaharias, by Elizabeth A. Lynn (Chelsea House Publishers, 1989); grades 6–10.

A Pictorial History of Women in America, by Ruth Warren (Crown Publishers, 1975); grades 7–9.